relaxed
aga
cooking

sarah whitaker

with photographs by

matthew leighton

Food preparation:
Sarah Whitaker
Food styling:
Sarah Whitaker and **Matthew Leighton**
*(all the photographs are of the actual recipes and
once we had finished, we ate the lot!)*
Photographs:
Matthew Leighton
Unit 8, The Old Dairy, Rushley Lane, Winchcombe,
Cheltenham, Gloucestershire, GL54 5JE
www.leightonstudios.com

There is probably no such thing as an original recipe. If I have
inadvertently duplicated anyone else's ideas, I apologise – sometimes I
think there must be a spy in Sarah's kitchen when I see a television cook
make a dish that I invented the day before!

Details of demonstrations, further copies of this book
and copies of Sarah's other recipe collections:
Home Made in Nether Wallop
and
The Twelve Days of Christmas
are available from:
The Trout, Nether Wallop, Hampshire, SO20 8EW
e mail: kitchen@sarahwhitaker.com
www.sarahwhitaker.com

relaxed

aga

cooking

sarah whitaker

with photographs by
matthew leighton

for Anthony, with love
and
for Daisy, Clementine and James, uncomplaining guinea pigs!

'Aga' and 'Rayburn' are registered trademarks of Aga Foodservice Group plc

'Bake-O-Glide'™ is a reusable non-stick, coated cooking material manufactured
by Falcon Products Ltd and available from cookshops and from Aga shops

First published in Great Britain in 2006 by
Sarah Whitaker
The Trout, Nether Wallop, Stockbridge, Hampshire, SO20 8EW
www.sarahwhitaker.com

Reprinted 2007

ISBN 13   978-0-9554306-0-2

Produced by Action Publishing Technology Ltd, Gloucester
Printed in Great Britain

contents

Getting to know your Aga   vi

Starters, soups and salads   2

Vegetables and vegetarian dishes   18

Fish   35

Poultry, meat and game   46

Puddings   78

Cakes and Baking   108

Sauces and basics   118

Index   121

getting to know your aga

It is perfectly possible to cook on an Aga for 30 years and never use any of the cast iron cooking techniques. Lots of people do. They may wonder why the cooker loses heat, but love the cooker so much that they don't mind, much. Then they learn a few simple techniques, keep the lids down and cook more in the ovens and – as if by magic – the cooker stops losing heat and they never look back. If this is you, read on . . .

Life with an Aga is like a friendship. Its warm, benign presence in the kitchen is such a comfort in the house. It will cook any food you want, quickly or slowly, perfectly. From a slow-roasted Christmas turkey to a piece of toast, it is the ultimate cooker. For some people, it is the cast iron monster in the kitchen, frightening in the extreme – all those doors and no visible controls, where on earth do you start?

Put simply, an Aga has two hot plates: the left hand *boiling plate*, is very hot – it boils. The right hand, *simmering plate*, is about half the temperature of the boiling plate – it simmers. The two-oven Aga has a top, *roasting oven*, which is very hot – it roasts, and a lower, *simmering oven* that is about half the temperature of the roasting oven – it simmers. The three-oven Aga has an additional *baking oven* that runs at a perfect temperature for baking, about half way between the roasting and simmering ovens. The four-oven Aga also has a *warming oven*, cooler than the simmering oven. And that's it.

The Aga is a heat storage cooker; it maintains heat until the lids are opened for too long or cool food is put into the ovens, when the thermostat kicks in and the heat gradually regenerates. 80% of all cooking on an Aga takes place in the ovens, saving heat and fuel. This has the added benefit of no spitting fat to clear up and no cooking smells – the ovens are vented to the flue and all smells just disappear up the chimney.

You should never need to turn it up or down – don't go near that dial, except to vacuum away the dog hairs occasionally! Please don't turn the Aga up if you are cooking for a party – you will only burn things, as it will be much hotter than you are used to! It may cook a little more slowly if the ovens are very full, but it will be consistent and reliable.

Many of these recipes refer to hanging the tins and shelves from the runners at the sides of the ovens. Always count the runners downwards from the top of the oven. Hanging roasting and baking tins from the runners uses less space – you can fit much more into the ovens at once!

a note about ingredients

I have deliberately not specified organic, free range or unrefined ingredients in my recipes. The choice is up to you, the cook.

I prefer to use good quality, seasonal, locally produced fresh ingredients, rather than those imported from around the world, out of season and context. I am not convinced that all imported 'organic' foods meet the strict UK standards. For example, I use local bacon in preference to imported pancetta, as I can see pigs in the fields nearby.

I will not use any ingredient that I cannot easily buy locally – it seems so unfair to say that a recipe will only work if you use particular herbs gathered by fairies in the Provençal moonlight or a certain brand of olive oil only available from one Italian delicatessen in a back street in Islington or through the internet!

That said, I am very fortunate to live on the Hampshire/Wiltshire border, where wonderful farmers' markets, fresh fish and traditional butchers are found in abundance.

preparing ahead

In many of these recipes I have said that the food can be prepared ahead – to be cooked and either kept warm, or cooled and reheated to eat later or the next day.

Many of these dishes freeze really well, either part-cooked, or ready to defrost and serve. I tend to wrap dishes for freezing in kitchen paper, which absorbs any liquid given off during defrosting, to save things from becoming watery.

This does not mean that you *have* to make things in advance, just that you can, if it suits you to do so.

chicken roulade with tarragon cream

Serves 6 – 10, depending upon how thick the slices are!

5 oz (150g) chicken breast

4 eggs

Salt and pepper

Filling:

1 tbsp chopped tarragon

8 oz (225g) cream cheese

2 oz (55g) sliced Parma ham

Oven temp:

Roasting oven, 190C, 375F, Gas 5

Prepare in advance:

Roulade will keep in the fridge for up to 24 hours

Freeze:

Yes, wrap the finished roulade in kitchen paper (to absorb any liquid given off as it thaws) before wrapping in cling film or a plastic bag to freeze

1 Set the cream cheese on the back of the Aga to soften. Line the large roasting tin with Bake-O-Glide.

2 Separate eggs and whizz the yolks, chicken and seasoning to a paste. Beat the whites until stiff then fold into the mixture.

3 Spread the mixture over the tin and hang from the lowest runners in the roasting oven for 8–10 minutes.

4 When the roulade is cooked, turn it out onto a clean tea towel, remove the Bake-O-Glide, roll in the tea towel and leave to cool.

5 Beat the cream cheese with the tarragon and seasoning.

6 Unroll the roulade and spread with the cheese filling. Lay on the slices of ham, then roll up tightly and chill for about an hour until set.

7 To serve, cut into 1" (2cms) slices and arrange on a plate, decorated with sprigs of tarragon.

Alternative flavours for the roulade:

1 *Try adding a whizzed salmon steak to the yolks instead of the chicken, then add a spoonful of dill sauce to the cream cheese before spreading it over the salmon roulade, lay on a few slices of smoked salmon and roll up.*

2 *Whizz a bunch of rocket and add to the yolks instead of the chicken and add sliced sun dried tomatoes to the cream cheese.*

soufflé mushrooms

Serves 4

4 large field mushrooms

1 egg

1 tbsp fresh parmesan

½ tsp Dijon mustard

Salt and pepper

Oven:

Roasting oven, 200C, 400F, Gas 6

Prepare in advance:

Assemble the mushrooms and keep in the fridge for 2 hours, uncooked

Prepare ahead:

Eat as soon as it is cooked

Freeze:

Not this one, the mushrooms become watery when they defrost

1 Line the small roasting tin with Bake-O-Glide.

2 Lay the mushrooms in the tin.

3 Separate the egg. Grate the parmesan. Mix together the egg yolk, grated cheese, mustard and seasoning. Whisk the egg white until firm then fold in to the mixture.

4 Pile the cheese soufflé mix into the mushrooms and hang the tin from the third set of runners in the roasting oven for 10–12 minutes until puffed up and golden.

5 Serve at once. Right now, quick before they collapse!

caramel pear salad

Serves 4

4 ripe pears

4 oz (110g) granulated sugar

2 tbsp water

1 oz (25g) pecan nuts

3 oz (95g) Roquefort cheese

Bag of mixed salad leaves

2 tbsp French dressing

Prepare in advance:

Prepare the pears up to an hour in advance

Prepare ahead:

Mix together up to an hour ahead, but do not dress the salad

Freeze:

No, the raw pears go rubbery in the freezer

1 Put the sugar and water into a heavy based pan and put onto the simmering plate. Slowly bring to the boil, swirling the pan around to dissolve the sugar. Once dissolved, boil for 8–10 minutes, until golden.

2 Meanwhile, peel, core and quarter the pears. Slice each quarter in half lengthways. Lay the slices onto a piece of Bake-O-Glide. Pour the caramel over the pears and leave to harden.

3 Just before serving, toss the salad leaves in the dressing and arrange on four plates. Pile the pear slices on top of the salad, scatter over the nuts and crumble the cheese over.

tomato-stuffed peppers

Serves 4

2 red peppers

12 cherry tomatoes

1 tbsp chopped lemon thyme

4 anchovy fillets

1 tbsp olive oil

2 cloves smoked garlic (or fresh garlic if unavailable)

$\frac{1}{2}$ tsp caster sugar

Salt and pepper

4 slices French bread

Oven:

Roasting oven, 200C, 400F, Gas 6

Prepare in advance:

Cook the dish, cool and keep in the fridge for a day, the peppers improve on keeping!

Prepare ahead:

Keep the cooked peppers warm beside the Aga for a couple of hours

Freeze:

No, everything goes very watery as it defrosts

1. Put a pan of water on to boil. Put the cherry tomatoes into a sieve then dip into the boiling water for a minute. Drop into a bowl of cold water then slip off the skins *(or don't bother and just use them unpeeled!).*

2. Cut the peppers in half lengthways and remove the seeds and membranes.

3. Chop the garlic with the anchovies and thyme, then divide the mixture between the pepper halves.

4. Put three cherry tomatoes into each pepper half, dribble a little olive oil over them, season with salt, pepper and sugar then put into a small roasting tin lined with Bake-O-Glide.

5. Hang from the second set of runners for about 25 minutes until cooked through.

6. Serve warm or tepid, on slices of French bread to soak up the juices.

choux puffs

Makes 20

¼ pint (150ml) water

2 oz (55g) butter

2½ oz (65g) plain flour

2 eggs

2 oz (55g) grated cheddar

Oven:

Roasting oven, 200C, 400F, Gas 6

Prepare in advance:

Mix together the choux pastry and keep in the fridge for up to 24 hours

Prepare ahead:

Keep the puffs warm in the simmering or warming oven for up to half an hour

Freeze:

Yes, defrost and reheat in the roasting oven for 5 minutes only

1 Put the cold plain shelf into the roasting oven to heat up.

2 Put the water and butter into a heavy based pan and slowly bring to the boil on the simmering plate. When it is boiling, tip in the flour and beat well. Off the heat, break in the eggs one at a time and beat well, then beat in the grated cheese.

3 Lay a sheet of Bake-O-Glide on the work surface and then either pipe or spoon blobs of the mixture onto the sheet.

4 Take the now hot shelf from the oven and slide on the Bake-O-Glide. Hang the shelf from the third set of runners and bake for 15 minutes until the pastry is golden and puffed up.

5 Serve warm, with a glass of wine.

stilton soufflé

Serves 6

4 oz (110g) stilton cheese

2¼ oz (60g) butter

2 oz (55g) plain flour

1 pint (550ml) milk

4 eggs

Salt and pepper

2 tbsp grated fresh parmesan cheese

Oven:

Roasting oven, 200C, 400F, Gas 6

Prepare in advance:

The prepared soufflé will keep in the fridge for up to 24 hours, but cook it at the last minute!

Prepare ahead:

Eat as soon as it is ready.

Freeze:

Yes, uncooked – make the soufflé up to the point of going into the oven, pour into prepared ramekins, cover with cling film and freeze. To cook, remove the film, set the dishes in a roasting tin and hang from the third set of runners in the roasting oven for about 20 minutes until defrosted, puffed up and browned.

1   Melt the butter in a pan on the simmering plate. Using a pastry brush, grease six ramekin dishes (or a 2 pint soufflé dish) with melted butter. Put some grated parmesan into each ramekin and shake around so that it sticks to the butter.

2   Add the flour to the remaining butter in the pan and once mixed, stir in the milk and seasoning. Bring to the boil on the simmering plate, stirring all the time as this is a very thick sauce. Set on one side to cool a little.

3   Crumble the cheese and beat into the cool sauce. Separate the eggs and stir the yolks into the sauce, one at a time. Whisk the egg whites until stiff, then fold in the cheese sauce.

4   Pour into the prepared dishes and set in the small roasting tin. Hang the tin from the third set of runners in the roasting oven for 15 minutes (if in one big dish, cook for 25 minutes) until puffed up and golden.

5   Serve immediately before it collapses!

hot halloumi and grape salad

Serves 4

8 oz (225g) halloumi cheese

6 oz (175g) seedless grapes

4 oz (115g) cherry tomatoes

6 oz (175g) mixed salad leaves

Dressing:

2 tbsp olive oil

1 tbsp lemon juice

½ tsp sugar

Salt and pepper

1 tbsp fresh thyme

Oven:

Simmering plate

Prepare in advance:

Get all the ingredients ready, but do not cook the cheese or dress the salad until you are ready to eat it.

Freeze: *Not this one*

1 Cut the cheese into thick slices. Remove the grapes from their stalks and mix all the dressing ingredients together in a clean jam jar.

2 Put a piece of Bake-O-Glide on the simmering plate. Lay the cheese slices onto the simmering plate for about 2–3 minutes, then turn and cook the other side.

3 Put the salad leaves and grapes into a bowl, pour the dressing over and toss well. Divide between four plates and top with the grilled cheese.

4 Serve at once.

nasturtium, rocket, strawberry and prawn salad

Serves 4

Handful nasturtium flowers

Bunch of rocket leaves

4 oz (110g) strawberries

4 oz (110g) cooked, peeled king prawns

3 tbsp olive oil

1 tbsp balsamic vinegar

Salt and pepper

Oven: none!

Prepare ahead:

Mix together half an hour early, but do not dress the salad until ready to serve it

Freeze:

No, unless you count using frozen prawns!

1 Trim and halve the strawberries (slice them if very large).

2 For the dressing: put the oil, vinegar and seasoning into a clean jam jar and shake well.

3 Put the rocket, strawberries, prawns and flowers into a bowl, pour over the dressing, toss briefly and serve at once with a slice of crusty bread to mop up any juices.

Not really an Aga-specific recipe, but delicious nonetheless!

asparagus and
pea soup

Serves 4

1 bunch – about 8 oz (225g) fresh English asparagus

12 oz (340g) fresh peas, shelled (or frozen)

1 pint (550ml) stock

8 spring onions

3 rashers streaky bacon

2 tbsp olive oil

2 slices white bread

3 tbsp double cream

Oven:

Simmering oven, 130C, 250F, Gas 1

Prepare in advance:

Keep the soup in the fridge for up to 24 hours

Prepare ahead:

Keep warm in the simmering or warming oven for half an hour

Freeze:

Yes

1 Bring the stock to the boil on the boiling plate.

2 Trim the spring onions and cut into ½" (1cm) slices.

3 Remove the asparagus tips and set aside. Cut the remaining asparagus into chunks and put into the stock, with the peas. Cover and put into the simmering oven for 15 minutes, until really tender. When cooked, puree in a processor or with a hand-blender. Season.

4 Snip the bacon into ½" (1cm) strips and cut the bread into ½" (1cm) cubes. Heat the oil in a frying pan on the boiling plate and add the bacon and bread and fry until brown and crispy, turning frequently.

5 Bring the soup back to the boil and add the reserved asparagus tips. Simmer on the simmering plate for 5 minutes while you are cooking the bacon.

6 Serve with a swirl of cream in each bowl and a scattering of fried bread and bacon.

parsnip and stilton soup

Serves 4 – 6

1 lb (450g) parsnips

1 tbsp olive oil

½ oz (15g) butter

2 pints (1 litre) stock

1 onion

2 medium potatoes

Salt and pepper

4 oz (110g) Stilton cheese

Oven:

Simmering oven, 130C, 350F, Gas 1

Prepare in advance:

Keep the cooled soup in the fridge for up to 24 hours

Prepare ahead:

Keep warm in the simmering or warming oven for half an hour

Freeze: Yes

1 Peel the parsnips, potatoes and onions, and cut into even sized pieces.

2 Melt the oil and butter together and add the onion. Cook on the boiling plate until sizzling and then cover and put into the simmering oven for 15 minutes to soften.

3 Stir in the parsnips and potatoes and then the stock. Bring to the boil then cover and put back into the simmering oven for about 25 minutes until the vegetables are soft.

4 Purée the soup, with the cheese, in a processor or liquidiser. Season, reheat gently without boiling, and serve.

creamy onion soup

Serves 4 - 6

3 medium onions

2 medium potatoes

1 oz (25g) butter

1 pint (550ml) stock

½ pint (275ml) creamy milk

Salt and pepper

To serve:

¼ pint (150ml) cream

2 tbsp chopped parsley

Oven:

Simmering oven, 130C, 250F, Gas 1

Prepare in advance:

As parsnip and stilton soup

smart mushroom soup

Serves 4 – 6

8 oz (225g) mushrooms

1½ pints (725ml) good stock

1 oz (25g) butter

1 medium onion

1 tbsp olive oil

2 cloves garlic

½ pint (275ml) cream

1 medium potato

½ pint (275ml) creamy milk

1 tsp ground cinnamon

Chopped parsley to garnish

Oven:

Simmering oven,

130C, 250F, Gas 1

Prepare in advance:

The cooled soup will keep in the fridge for a couple of days.

Prepare ahead:

Keep the soup warm in the simmering or warming oven for up to an hour, add the topping at the last minute before serving.

Freeze:

Yes, before adding the cream or frothy milk topping

1   Peel and finely chop the onion and garlic. Melt the butter and oil together in a heavy based pan on the boiling plate and add the onion and garlic. Stir over the heat for a couple of minutes until cooked (do not allow to brown too much). Peel and dice the potato, then add it to the onion mixture. Finely chop the mushrooms (a processor is perfect for this) and add to the pan.

2   Stir in the stock, bring to the boil then cover and transfer to the simmering oven for 25 minutes.

3   Whizz briefly in a food processor, then return to the pan, stir in the cream and pour into individual bowls.

4   Put the milk into a pan and bring to the boil. Using a cappuccino frother, froth the milk and then spoon on top of each bowl.

5   Sprinkle on a little cinnamon and some parsley and serve at once.

You don't have to add the frothy milk if it is too much bother, the soup is good on its own, but the finishing touch makes it into something special.

roasted butternut
squash soup

Serves 4 – 6

1 butternut squash

3 medium potatoes

1 medium onion

1 clove garlic

2 tbsp olive oil

2 pints (1 litre) stock

To garnish:

Croutons

3 tbsp double cream

Chopped parsley

Oven:

Roasting oven, 200C, 400F, Gas 6
and simmering oven, 130C, 250F,
Gas 1

Prepare in advance:

The cooled soup will keep in the
fridge for up to 24 hours

Prepare ahead:

Will keep warm in the simmering
oven for an hour

Freeze:

Yes

1   Cut the squash in half and set it into a roasting tin,
    lined with Bake-O-Glide. Dribble over a spoonful of
    oil, hang the tin from the third set of runners in the
    roasting oven and roast the squash for about an hour,
    until it has caramelised at the edges and is soft.
    Remove from the oven and allow to cool a little.

2   Meanwhile, peel and chop the onion, crush the garlic
    and cut the potatoes into 1" (2cms) cubes. Heat the
    remaining oil in a heavy based pan on the simmering
    plate, stir in the onion, garlic and potato and heat
    until sizzling, then cover and transfer to the simmering
    oven for 20 minutes or so, to soften without
    colouring.

3   When the onion, garlic and potatoes are soft, add the
    stock, season well and bring to the boil. Once
    boiling, cover and return to the simmering oven for a
    further 20 minutes.

4   When the squash is cool enough to handle, scoop the
    flesh out of the skin and add to the pan of soup.
    Using a hand blender, whizz together – either leaving
    a few chunks of vegetable or until it is smooth, as you
    prefer – and serve with a scattering of croutons, a
    swirl of cream and a bit of parsley on the top.

aga-baked
tomato tart

Serves 4 – 6

1 packet (375g) ready-rolled puff pastry

8 tomatoes

2 tbsp olive oil

Salt and pepper

1 tsp caster sugar

1 egg, beaten

4 oz (110g) Cheshire cheese or goats' cheese or feta, depending upon how strong you like it!

2 tbsp fresh pesto

Handful black olives (optional)

Oven:

Roasting oven, 200C, 400F, Gas 6

Prepare in advance:

The tomatoes will keep in the fridge for several days

Prepare ahead:

Keep the tart warm in the simmering or warming oven for up to half an hour

Freeze:

Tomatoes only

1 Halve the tomatoes and lay them cut side up in the small roasting tin, lined with Bake-O-Glide. Dribble the oil over the tomatoes, scatter with salt, pepper and sugar. Put into the simmering oven to dry out for about 3 to 4 hours, depending upon how big they are. Remove from the oven and allow to cool.

2 Unroll the pack of pastry onto a sheet of Bake-O-Glide on the plain shelf. Using a sharp knife, score a shallow line about 1" (2cms) from the edge. Brush the pastry with beaten egg.

3 Spread the pesto over the inside of the pastry 'frame'. Either crumble the Cheshire or feta cheese, or slice up the goats' cheese and scatter over the pastry.

4 Put the tomato halves, cut side up on top, add a few black olives if you like, then hang the plain shelf from the lowest set of runners in the roasting oven for about 10 minutes, until puffed up and golden.

5 Serve at once, with some bread to mop up the tomato juices.

Alternative: Cut the pastry into individual-sized squares or rounds and make separate tarts. Or use filo pastry to make individual tartlets.

couscous and vegetable salad

Serves 4 – 6

9 oz (250g) couscous

7 fl oz (180ml) cold water

Good handful of parsley

Good handful of coriander

1 tbsp harissa paste

3 tbsp olive oil

2 tbsp lemon juice

Salt and pepper

2 courgettes

6 patty pans (optional)

A few sugar snap peas

A few spears of asparagus

3 spring onions

Oven temp:

Floor of roasting oven

Prepare in advance:

Prepare all the vegetables and keep in the fridge for up to 24 hours before cooking

Prepare ahead:

The salad will keep in the fridge for up to 12 hours

Freeze:

No

1 Put the couscous into a bowl and pour on the water. Leave to absorb the water for a few minutes.

2 Heat one tablespoon of the oil in a heavy based frying pan.

3 Cut all the vegetables into even sized pieces and toss in the oil. Place on the floor of the roasting oven and cook for 5 minutes. Shake the pan to turn them and return to the oven for a further couple of minutes.

4 Make the dressing: chop the herbs mix together the remaining oil, vinegar, harissa and seasoning with the herbs. Add to the couscous and mix well.

5 Add the cooked vegetables and serve either tepid or cold.

three cheese and poppy seed tart

Serves 4 – 6

6 oz (175g) plain flour

3 oz (75g) butter

1 tbsp parmesan cheese

1 tbsp poppy seeds

2–3 tbsp water

4 oz (110g) feta cheese

3 eggs

5 fl oz (150ml) milk

4 oz (110g) cheddar cheese

Salt and pepper

Oven:

Roasting oven, 200C, 400F, Gas 6

Prepare in advance:

The cooked, cooled tart will keep in the fridge for 24 hours

Prepare ahead:

Keep the tart warm in the simmering or warming oven for up to an hour

Freeze: *Yes, either the uncooked pastry in the dish or the complete cooked tart*

1 To make the pastry, put the flour, butter, poppy seeds and parmesan into a processor and whizz until the texture of breadcrumbs. With the motor running, add the water a spoonful (10ml) at a time until it comes together as a dough.

2 Roll out the pastry and line a 9" (23cms) ceramic flan dish. Chill or freeze until required.

3 For the filling, roughly chop the feta and put it into the pastry case. Grate the cheddar cheese into the pastry case. Put the eggs and milk into a bowl with a little salt and pepper and beat together.

4 Pour into the prepared flan case and put onto the floor of the roasting oven for about 25 minutes until set and golden.

More ideas for vegetarian tarts; they are so easy in the Aga. Roll out some pastry, line a 9" (23cms) ceramic dish and fill with:

pear and leek tart

Serves 4 – 6

3 ripe pears (or use tinned!)

3 leeks

3 eggs

5 fl oz (150ml) milk

Salt and pepper

2 tbsp pine nuts

1 Peel, core and quarter the pears; trim the leeks and cut into 2" long chunks, then slice the chunks in half lengthways. Melt the butter in a pan on the simmering plate and add the leeks and pears. When sizzling, cover and transfer to the simmering oven for 10 minutes until soft. Remove from the oven and allow to cool a little.

2 Spread half of the pear and leek mixture onto the pastry. Whizz the rest with the eggs and pour into the pastry case. Scatter the nuts over the top and then put onto the floor of the roasting oven for 25 minutes until set and golden.

pear, stilton and walnut tart

Serves 4 – 6

2 ripe pears (or use tinned!)

4 oz (110g) blue stilton cheese

2 oz (55g) walnut halves

3 eggs

5 fl oz (150ml) milk

Salt and pepper

This is a lovely Christmas alternative – it makes a change from stuffed peppers or nut roast, which seem to be the standard fare on offer to vegetarians!

1   Peel and halve the pears; remove the cores. Lay the pears onto the pastry and arrange the walnuts between them. Crumble the cheese over the walnuts. Mix together the eggs and milk with a little salt and pepper.

2   Pour into the prepared flan case and put onto the floor of the roasting oven for 25 minutes until set and golden.

chestnut, gorgonzola and sorrel tart

Serves 4 – 6

6 oz (175g) prepared chestnuts

Handful fresh sorrel

3 oz (75g) gorgonzola

3 eggs

1/2 pint (225ml) milk

Salt and pepper

1   Tip the chestnuts into the prepared flan case and scatter over the sorrel leaves. Crumble the cheese on top.

2   Mix the eggs and milk with a little salt and pepper. Pour into the prepared flan case and put onto the floor of the roasting oven for 25 minutes until set and golden.

mushroom tart

Serves 4 – 6

1/2 oz (10g) butter

6 oz (175g) mushrooms

2 spring onions

3 oz (75g) grated cheddar

3 eggs

1/2 pint (225ml) milk

Salt and pepper

1   Trim and slice the spring onions, wipe and slice the mushrooms. Grate the cheese. Melt the 1/2 oz butter in a pan and add the mushrooms.

2   Cook on the simmering plate until the juices run, then boil hard on the floor of the roasting oven for a couple of minutes, so that the juices boil away. Leave to cool. Tip the cool mushrooms into the prepared flan case, scatter over the spring onions and cheese.

3   Mix the eggs and milk with a little salt and pepper. Pour into a prepared pastry case and put onto the floor of the roasting oven for 25 minutes until set and golden.

mexican vegetable and bean stew

Serves 4 teenagers or 6 adults!

2 red onions

2 cloves garlic

2 medium potatoes

2 tbsp olive oil

2 large tins (400g each) red kidney beans

1 large tin (400g) chopped tomatoes

1/4 pint (150ml) tomato passata

8 oz (225g) tiny button mushrooms

1 tsp cocoa powder

1 tsp ground coriander

1 tsp smoked paprika

1/2 tsp chilli powder

Salt and pepper

Juice of half a lime

1 tbsp chopped fresh coriander

Oven:

Simmering oven,

130C, 250F, Gas 1

Prepare in advance:

Keep the cooked, cooled stew in the fridge for up to 24 hours

Prepare ahead:

Stew will keep warm in the simmering oven for an hour

Freeze:

Yes

1 Peel and chop the onions, peel and crush the garlic. Cut the potatoes into 1" (2cms) cubes. Drain the beans.

2 Heat the oil in a heavy based pan on the simmering plate, add the onions and garlic, potatoes and spices. Stir over the heat until sizzling, then cover and transfer to the simmering oven for 15 minutes to soften.

3 Put the pan back onto the simmering plate, then add the beans, tomatoes, mushrooms, cocoa and passata. Season well, bring to the boil then cover and return to the simmering oven for 25 minutes.

4 Just before serving, add the lime juice and chopped coriander. Serve with rice.

mushroom, leek and chickpea crumble

Serves 4

6 oz (175g) button mushrooms

2 medium leeks

8 oz (225g) chickpeas

1 oz (25g) butter

1 tbsp olive oil

1 oz (25g) plain flour

½ pint (275ml) milk

1 oz (25g) grated cheddar cheese

1 oz (25g) fresh breadcrumbs

1 oz (25g) pecan nuts, chopped

Oven:

Roasting oven, 200C, 400F, Gas 6

Prepare in advance:

Keep the cooked crumble in the fridge for up to 24 hours

Prepare ahead:

Will keep warm for 1 hour in the simmering or warming oven

Freeze:

Yes, defrost then warm through in the roasting oven for 15–20 minutes

1 Wash the chickpeas and soak in cold water for 4 hours or overnight. Next day, drain and cover with fresh water. Bring to the boil, boil hard for 10 minutes then cover and put into the simmering oven for 2 hours, until soft. Drain. (Alternatively, open a tin of chickpeas and continue . . .) .

2 Melt the butter and oil in a large pan. Trim and slice the leeks, quarter the mushrooms. Cook the leeks and mushrooms on the boiling plate until sizzling, then cover and put into the simmering oven for 20 minutes until soft.

3 For the crumble: mix together the grated cheese, breadcrumbs and chopped nuts.

4 Stir the chickpeas and flour into the pan of leeks and mushrooms, then blend in the milk. Cook on the simmering plate, stirring continuously, until boiling.

5 Turn into an ovenproof dish then scatter over the crumble mixture. Bake in the centre of the roasting oven for 15–20 minutes until bubbling and golden.

Omit the pecan nuts if you have an allergy, the taste is as good, but the topping is not as crunchy!

Just add some salad to make a complete and delicious meal.

leek and onion gougère

*Serves 4 as a main course,
6 as a starter*

¼ pint (140ml) water

2 oz (55g) butter

2½ oz (65g) plain flour

2 eggs

2 oz (55g) grated cheddar

1 tbsp olive oil

2 medium leeks

1 onion

4 oz (110g) cream cheese

1 tbsp grainy mustard

salt and pepper

Oven:

Simmering oven,

130C, 250F, Gas 1,

then roasting oven, 200C, 400F,

Gas 6

Prepare in advance:

Make the choux pastry and keep
in the fridge for up to 24 hours;
the filling will also keep overnight
in the fridge, assemble just before
cooking

Prepare ahead:

Keep warm in the simmering or
warming oven for half an hour

Freeze:

*Yes, defrost then warm through in
the roasting oven for 10 minutes*

1 Set the cream cheese onto the back of the Aga to soften.

2 Peel and slice the onion and leeks. Heat the oil in a heavy pan and add the onion and leeks and cook on the simmering plate until sizzling. Cover and put into the simmering oven to continue cooking for 15 minutes.

3 Remove the onions and leeks from the simmering oven, uncover and put onto the boiling plate for a couple of minutes to boil off any excess juices. Stir in the cream cheese and mustard, season well and set aside to cool.

4 Put the water and butter into a heavy based pan and slowly bring to the boil on the simmering plate. When it is boiling, tip in the flour and beat well. Off the heat, break in the eggs one at a time and beat well, then beat in half of the grated cheese.

5 Line a baking sheet with Bake-O-Glide and then spoon blobs of the mixture to form a circle on the sheet. Pile the leek and onion mixture into the centre and sprinkle the remaining grated cheese on top.

6 Hang the sheet from the third set of runners and bake for 25–30 minutes until the pastry is golden and puffed up.

7 Serve at once, with a tomato salad and some crusty bread.

chestnut, mushroom and sage pasta

Serves 4

12 oz (375g) fresh pasta quills

2 oz (55g) butter

1 tbsp olive oil

4 large field mushrooms or 12 oz (375g) mixed mushroom selection

1 clove garlic

Handful fresh sage leaves

1 pack peeled chestnuts (200g)

Small tub (200g) crème fraîche

2 tbsp grated fresh parmesan

Oven:

Floor of roasting oven

Prepare in advance:

This is so quick to chuck together, there is no need!

Prepare ahead:

Pasta and sauce will keep in the simmering or warming oven for 15 minutes

Freeze:

No, the mushrooms go rubbery and the pasta sticks together as it defrosts

1 Melt the butter and oil together in a wide pan on the simmering plate.

2 Slice the mushrooms and crush the garlic. Toss in the butter and oil on the simmering plate for a few seconds then transfer to the floor of the roasting oven to fry for 5 minutes until golden.

3 Bring a large pan of water to the boil and tip in the pasta. Keep on the boiling plate and cook according to packet instructions.

4 Snip the sage into the mushroom pan and tip in the chestnuts and crème fraîche. Cook for a further minute or two, until beginning to brown. Drain the pasta and add to the mushroom pan.

5 Season and scatter over the parmesan before serving.

6 You may prefer to cook the pasta in the simmering oven – just bring it to a brisk boil in plenty of water, cover and cook for as long as the packet instructs.

mushroom risotto

Serves 4

8 oz (half a pint in a measuring jug) (225g) risotto rice

1 medium onion

2 cloves garlic

2 tbsp olive oil

1 oz (25g) butter

1 packet (50g) dried mushrooms

4 oz pack (125g) mixed exotic fresh mushrooms

$3/4$ pint (400ml) stock

2 tbsp white wine

Salt and pepper

3 tbsp grated fresh parmesan cheese

Parsley to garnish

Oven:

Simmering oven,

130C, 250F, Gas 1

Prepare in advance:

Will keep in the fridge for up to 24 hours, reheat in roasting oven for 25 minutes in a covered dish

Prepare ahead:

Will keep warm for up to an hour in the simmering oven

Freeze:

Yes

1 Soak the dried mushrooms in about $1/4$ pint (150ml) boiling water for an hour to rehydrate.

2 Peel and chop the onion, crush the garlic.

3 Heat the oil in a heavy pan on the simmering plate, and add the onion and garlic. When sizzling, cover and put into the simmering oven for 15 minutes to soften.

4 Stir the rice into the cooked onions, add the wine, stock and the dried mushrooms with their soaking liquor to the pan. Bring to the boil, then cover and return to the simmering oven for at least 30 minutes.

5 Slice the fresh mushrooms and put into a pan with the butter. Cook on the simmering plate for 5 minutes until tender.

6 Stir the fresh mushrooms into the risotto, with the parmesan, then serve with a scattering of chopped parsley.

rice and tomato salad

Serves 6

1 medium onion

1 clove garlic

1 tbsp olive oil

$1/2$ pint (225g) long grain rice

$3/4$ pint (425ml) stock or water

1 tbsp sun dried tomato purée

6 half cooked tomatoes (see recipe, page 119)

3 fresh tomatoes

3 tbsp French dressing

Salt and pepper

Fresh basil leaves

Oven:

Simmering oven,

130C, 250F, Gas 1

Prepare in advance:

Will keep in the fridge for up to 24 hours

Freeze:

Not with the fresh tomatoes in, they go watery; otherwise yes, defrost and reheat in the roasting oven for 20-25 minutes

This is just as good hot, as a warming risotto, as it is cold as a salad.

1 Peel and chop the onion and crush the garlic. Chop the sun dried tomatoes.

2 Heat the oil in a large pan on the simmering plate and add the tomatoes, onion and garlic. When sizzling, cover and put into the simmering oven for 10 minutes to soften.

3 Take the cooked onion from the oven and stir in the rice, tomato purée, cooked tomatoes and stock. Bring to the boil then cover and return to the simmering oven for 15 minutes.

4 Meanwhile, roughly chop the fresh tomatoes.

5 Take the cooked rice from the oven and leave to cool for 5 minutes. Stir in the French dressing and fresh tomatoes and then serve warm or chill and serve cold, scattered with torn basil leaves.

Plain rice is cooked in just the same way in the Aga. Measure the volume of the rice and put it into a pan, add one and a half times as much water, bring to the boil, cover and cook in the simmering oven for 15 minutes. Stir in some chopped parsley and butter just before serving plain rice.

instant pasta

Serves 4 adults or 2 teenagers

12 oz (375g) dried pasta

7 oz (200g) tub cream cheese

2 tbsp pesto sauce from a jar

1 tbsp fresh parmesan, grated

Oven:

Boiling plate

Prepare in advance:

No need, this is meant to be
instant!

Prepare ahead:

Keep in the simmering or warming
oven for 10 minutes

Freeze:

*Probably not, pasta sticks together
as it defrosts*

As close to instant as you can get!

1 Set the cream cheese on the back of the Aga to soften while the pasta cooks.

2 Put a large pan of water on the boiling plate and when it is boiling, tip in the pasta. Stir around and transfer to the simmering plate for 12 minutes (or as instructed by the packet) until cooked.

3 Drain the pasta. Put the cream cheese into the still-warm, empty pan, add the pesto sauce and set on the simmering plate. Stir around to melt the cheese, then tip in the drained pasta.

4 Stir to mix and serve at once, with a sprinkling of grated parmesan on top.

This works well with sun dried tomato purée or any other pasta sauce from a jar instead of the pesto.

ratatouille and lentil crumble

Serves 4

1 aubergine

2 red peppers

2 medium courgettes

2 tbsp olive oil

1 onion

2 cloves garlic

1 tin (400g) chopped tomatoes

Handful fresh basil leaves

1/2 tsp balsamic vinegar

Salt and pepper

3 oz (75g) red lentils

Crumble topping:

2 oz (55g) fresh breadcrumbs

2 oz (55g) grated cheddar cheese

1 tbsp chopped fresh parsley

Oven:

Roasting oven, 200C, 400F, Gas 6

Prepare in advance:

Keep the cooked crumble in the fridge for up to 24 hours

Prepare ahead:

Keep warm in the simmering or warming oven for an hour or so

Freeze:

Yes, defrost and warm through in the roasting oven for 20–25 minutes

1 Wash the vegetables, then cut the aubergine, peppers, courgettes and onion into even sized pieces. Crush the garlic.

2 Heat the oil in a heavy based ovenproof deep sauté pan and tip in the vegetables. When sizzling, set on the floor of the roasting oven for 10 minutes, shaking occasionally to turn the vegetables.

3 Once they have browned, tip in the tin of tomatoes, lentils, seasoning and vinegar. Bring to the boil, then cover and put into the simmering oven for about 30 minutes, until the lentils have cooked.

4 Mix together the crumble ingredients. Tear the basil leaves into the ratatouille and mix well, then tip into an ovenproof serving dish, scatter the crumble over the top and cook at the top of the roasting oven for 15 minutes until the topping is melted and browned.

mushroom stroganoff

Serves 4 as a starter, 2 as a main course

12 oz (375g) button mushrooms

½ oz (15g) butter

1 tbsp walnut oil

1 clove garlic

1 tbsp sun dried tomato purée

1 tbsp grainy mustard

Small tub (150ml) crème fraîche

Salt and pepper

1 tbsp chopped fresh parsley

Oven:

Floor of roasting oven

Prepare in advance:

Keep the stroganoff in the fridge for up to 24 hours, reheat gently!

Prepare ahead:

Keep warm in the simmering or warming oven for up to an hour

Freeze:

No, the mushrooms go soggy

I made a huge bucket of this as the vegetarian alternative for a chilli evening in Nether Wallop – the whole panful disappeared very quickly!

1   Quarter the mushrooms, peel and crush the garlic.

2   Melt the oil and butter together in a pan on the simmering plate, add the mushrooms and garlic. Stir around to coat with the oil and butter, then transfer to the floor of the roasting oven for about 5 minutes. Shake the pan and cook for a further 5 minutes, until the juices have mostly boiled away.

3   Stir in the tomato purée, mustard and crème fraîche. Season well and bring to the boil on the simmering plate.

4   Serve scattered with chopped parsley - with chunks of bread as a starter or on a bed of rice as a main course.

To serve as a main course, add Aga rice (see page 26) and some salad.

roasted roots

Serves 8

1 lb (450g) King Edward potatoes

2 medium sized sweet potatoes

6 large parsnips

1 oz (25g) goose fat, dripping or
1 tbsp sunflower oil

1 tbsp plain flour

Oven:

Roasting oven, 200C, 400F, Gas 6

Prepare in advance:

The roasted vegetables will keep
in the fridge for up to 24 hours or
on the worktop near the Aga for
an hour

Prepare ahead:

Allow the roasted vegetables to
cool completely, then reheat in the
roasting oven for 5 minutes

Freeze:

*YES! Reheat from frozen at the top
of the roasting oven for 15–20
minutes*

1   If using dripping or goose fat, set in a bowl on the back of the Aga to melt.

2   Line a small shallow baking tin with Bake-O-Glide.

3   Peel the potatoes, sweet potatoes and parsnips and cut into even sized pieces. Put into a pan of cold water. Cover, bring to the boil, and simmer for a minute. Drain then add the flour. Put on the lid and shake well, then pour in the fat, cover and shake again.

4   Tip the coated vegetables into the tin and hang from the second set of runners and cook for about 45 minutes to an hour, until crisp and golden.

Roasted root vegetables reheat brilliantly in the Aga. Cook them in advance and allow to cool before chilling or freezing them. When ready to serve, just tip them into a roasting tin (no extra fat is needed) and hang from the second set of runners. Chilled, they take about 5–10 minutes; from frozen about 15–20 minutes – making mass catering simple!

aga potato salad

Serves 4 – 6

1½ lbs (600g) new potatoes

2 tbsp olive oil

1 tbsp white wine vinegar

1 tsp grainy mustard

½ tsp light brown sugar

Salt and pepper

2 tbsp chopped chives

1 tbsp chopped parsley

2 tbsp mayonnaise
(optional)

Oven:

Simmering oven,

130C, 250F, Gas 1

Prepare in advance:

Salad will keep in the fridge for up
to 24 hours

Prepare ahead:

Make the potato salad an hour
before you want to eat, to allow it
time to cool down

Freeze:

*No, the potatoes go rubbery as
they defrost*

1　Put the potatoes into a pan and cover with water. Set
on the boiling plate and bring to the boil. When the
potatoes are boiling hard, drain them, cover with a lid
and put into the simmering oven for 25 minutes until
tender.

2　For the dressing, mix the oil, vinegar, mustard, sugar
and seasoning in a clean jam jar and shake until
mixed.

3　Remove the potatoes from the oven, drain again then
pour in the oil and vinegar dressing. Replace the lid
and shake well. Leave to cool.

4　When the potatoes are cool, stir in the chopped herbs
(and mayonnaise if using) and chill until serving.

*This method of cooking applies to all root vegetables –
potatoes, carrots, parsnips, celeriac, sweet potatoes,
swedes, turnips, etc – just bring them to a brisk boil,
drain away **all** the water, cover and cook in the
simmering oven until tender. The potatoes cook in their
own steam and you keep all the flavour and goodness
inside the vegetables.*

stilton mash

Serves 4

1½ lb (600g) potatoes

¼ pint (150ml) creamy milk

1 oz (25g) butter

2 oz (50g) stilton

Salt and pepper

Grated nutmeg

Oven:

Simmering oven,

130C, 250F, Gas 1

Prepare in advance:

Cooked, cooled mash will keep in the fridge for up to 24 hours, reheat in the roasting oven for 15 minutes

Prepare ahead:

Mash will keep warm for up to an hour in the simmering or warming oven

Freeze:

Yes, defrost and reheat in the Roasting oven for 15–20 minutes

1   Cut the potatoes into even sized pieces. Put into a pan and cover with water. Bring to the boil on the boiling plate, drain, cover and put into the simmering oven for 35–45 minutes until soft. Drain again.

2   Mash, then add the milk, butter, salt, pepper and a good grating of nutmeg, then crumble in the stilton. Beat with a wooden spoon until smooth and serve.

Other mash ideas:

Add a dollop of grainy mustard to the mashed potatoes instead of the cheese.

Stir in some pesto to make green mash.

*I **never** peel potatoes for mashing (unless they are very wrinkled!) – you lose so much of the goodness and fibre by removing the skin, as well as it being a time-consuming effort.*

The first time you produce mashed potatoes with shreds of skin in, it is greeted with cries of outrage. The second time, with acceptance, the third time it is completely normal, to the extent that my little treasures now greet white mashed potato with cries of 'Smash!!'

three vegetable mash

Serves 4–6

1 lb (450g) potatoes

½ lb (225g) celeriac

½ lb (225g) sweet potatoes

½ pint (275ml) creamy milk

1 oz (25g) butter

Salt, pepper and nutmeg

1   Cut the vegetables into even sized pieces – you may want to peel the celeriac.

2   Put the milk and butter in a mug and set on the back of the Aga to warm through.

3   Put all the vegetables into a pan and cover with water. Set onto the boiling plate and bring to the boil. Once boiling hard, drain off all the water, cover tightly and put into the simmering oven for about half an hour until tender.

three vegetable mash *continued*

Oven:

Simmering oven,
130C, 250F, Gas 1

Prepare in advance:

Cooked, cooled mash will keep in
the fridge for up to 24 hours,
reheat in the roasting oven for 15
minutes

Prepare ahead:

Will keep warm for up to an hour

Freeze:

Yes

4   Mash the vegetables with the warm milk, season well
and serve.

aga sauté potatoes

Serves 4

1 lb (450g) white potatoes
2 tbsp olive oil
Salt and pepper
1 tsp mixed dried herbs

Oven:

Simmering oven,
130C, 250F, Gas 1, then
roasting oven, 200C, 400F, Gas 6

Prepare in advance:

Cooked, cooled potatoes will keep
in the fridge for up to 24 hours

Prepare ahead:

Keep warm in the simmering or
warming oven for up to 1 hour

Freeze:

Yes, reheat in the roasting oven for 10 minutes

1   Put the potatoes into a heavy based pan and bring to
the boil. Drain and place, covered, in the simmering
oven for 20 minutes until just soft.

2   Remove the potatoes from the oven. Cut into even
sized pieces and return to the pan. Add the oil and
seasonings, and shake together.

3   Pour into a large roasting tin, lined with Bake-O-Glide,
and hang from the second set of runners and bake for
20–25 minutes, shaking occasionally to turn the
potatoes.

4   Serve when evenly browned and crisp.

farah's potato and aubergine curry

Serves 4, or more as an accompaniment

- 1 lb potatoes
- 1 medium aubergine
- 3 tomatoes
- 2 tbsp sunflower oil
- 1/2 tsp mustard seeds
- 1/2 tsp cumin seeds
- 1/2 tsp ground cumin
- 1/2 tsp ground coriander
- 1/2 tsp (or more to taste) chilli powder
- 1 tbsp sun dried tomato purée
- 1/2 tsp salt

Oven:

Simmering oven 130C, 250F, Gas 1

then

roasting oven, 200C, 400F, Gas 6

Prepare in advance:

Will keep in the fridge for up to 24 hours

Prepare ahead:

Keep warm in the simmering oven for half an hour

Freeze:

Don't see why not!

1   Cut the potatoes, aubergines and tomatoes into even-sized cubes, about 1" (2.5cms) across.

2   Put the oil, mustard seeds and cumin seeds into a heavy based pan on the simmering plate and cover with a lid. When the seeds begin to pop, remove from the heat and stir in the rest of the spices, tomato purée and salt. Stir over the heat for a minute or two, then add the potatoes, aubergines and tomatoes. Stir in the water and bring to the boil on the boiling plate. When boiling hard, cover and put into the simmering oven to continue cooking for at least 3/4 hour until the vegetables are tender.

3   Remove from the oven, remove the lid and put the pan onto the floor of the roasting oven to boil off the excess water – about 5–10 minutes.

salmon en croûte

Serves 6–8

1 whole salmon, about 4 lbs (2kg)

1 bunch, about 8 oz (225g) fresh English asparagus

6 oz (175g) cream cheese

2 tbsp chopped fresh dill

1lb (450g) puff pastry – or two 375g sheets of ready rolled

1 egg

Salt and pepper

Oven:

Roasting oven, 200C, 400F, Gas 6

Prepare in advance:

The fish will keep in its pastry case in the fridge for up to 24 hours

Prepare ahead:

Cook the fish and serve tepid or keep in the fridge overnight

Freeze:

Yes, before it is cooked, or the pastry gets a bit fatty. Defrost and bake as usual

This is a very exciting dish, which caused my husband to propose, so you make it at your own risk!

1 Get your fishmonger to fillet and skin the salmon, or struggle with it yourself!

2 Set the cream cheese onto the back of the Aga to soften.

3 Bring a pan of water to the boil and cook the asparagus for 5 minutes until tender. Drain, and plunge into a bowl of cold water. Drain again and refill the bowl with more cold water. The asparagus should be completely cold by now.

4 Roll out half of the pastry (or unroll one of the sheets) and lay it on a piece of Bake-O-Glide on the plain shelf. Brush the outer edge – about an inch wide – with beaten egg.

5 Lay one of the pieces of salmon on top of the pastry. Spread with the cream cheese, then sprinkle over the dill, salt and pepper. Lay on the asparagus, then cover with the other piece of salmon, making sure that the tail end of one is above the head end of the other. This ensures that every slice has the same amount of salmon in it!

6 Roll out the rest of the pastry to fit the parcel, trimming to fit neatly. Lay the 'lid' onto the salmon and pinch the edges together. Brush with beaten egg, and decorate with some pastry trimmings. Brush again with egg over the trimmings, then hang the shelf from the third set of runners and bake for 20–25 minutes, until puffed up and golden. If the pastry is getting too brown, cover with foil.

7 Serve warm, with new potatoes and peas and hollandaise sauce, or cold with salad and mayonnaise.

plaice fillets with lime sauce

Serves 4, or 8 as a starter

4 plaice, filleted (or chunks of cod loin fillet)

Salt and pepper

2 tbsp butter

Sauce:

½ (275ml) pint fish stock

1 lime

1 tbsp cornflour

2 egg yolks

½ tsp caster sugar

Salt and pepper

Pinch ground ginger

1 tbsp chopped chives

Oven:

Roasting oven, 200C, 400F, Gas 6

Prepare in advance:

Assemble the fish and keep, covered, in the fridge for up to 12 hours before cooking

Prepare ahead:

Keep warm for up to 30 minutes

Freeze:

The fish, yes, but not the sauce

1 Line a roasting tin with Bake-O-Glide. Wash the fish fillets and pat dry on kitchen paper. Season then roll up the fillets (skin side on the inside) and lay them, folded side down, in the roasting tin.

2 Put a blob of butter on each piece of fish, grate on the rind of the lime, and cover the tin with foil. Hang the tin from the third set of runners and cook for about 15 minutes.

3 Remove from the tin and keep warm in the simmering oven until needed.

4 For the sauce: Pour the fish stock into the tin. Put onto the floor of the roasting oven to boil and reduce for 5 minutes. Squeeze the lime juice into a bowl and stir in the cornflour. Add to the stock, stir well and return to the oven floor for a further 5 minutes to cook and thicken the cornflour. Stir again.

5 Put the eggs, sugar, seasoning and ginger into a bowl and beat well. Still beating, pour on the hot sauce, which will thicken.

6 Serve the fish with the sauce poured over, and sprinkled with chives.

garlic tuna steaks

Serves 4

4 tuna steaks

2 oz (55g) butter

2 cloves garlic

2 tbsp chopped chives

Juice of a lemon

Salt and pepper

Oven:

Boiling plate

Prepare in advance:

This is so quick there is no need!

Prepare ahead:

Keep the tuna warm in simmering
or warming oven for up to 20
minutes

Freeze:

*Not this one. Cooked tuna ends up tasting like tinned
when it defrosts*

1   Put a cast iron or removable-handle griddle pan into
the roasting oven to heat up for a few minutes.

2   Transfer the pan to the boiling plate. Drop the steaks
into the griddle pan and cook on the boiling plate for
about 3 minutes each side, turning only once, then
set aside to rest.

3   Melt the butter in the pan with the garlic, lemon juice
and chives. Stir over the heat until foaming, then
pour over the tuna steaks and serve at once.

marinated
monkfish kebabs

Serves 4

1 lb (450g) monkfish tail

2 onions

2 red peppers

1 tbsp Thai fish sauce

1 tbsp sesame oil

2 Thai lime leaves

1 clove garlic, crushed

Salt and pepper

1   Soak four wooden skewers in water.

2   Cut the fish into 1½" (3cms) chunks. Peel and
quarter the onion and cut the pepper into 2" (5cms)
chunks.

3   Thread the fish, onion and pepper onto the skewers,
alternating each. Mix together the oil, fish sauce,
garlic and seasoning – you could add an optional
chopped red chilli if you like – and crumble in the lime
leaves. Pour this marinade over the fish skewers and
lay on a shallow baking dish, cover and refrigerate for
a couple of hours for the flavours to mingle.

marinated monkfish kebabs *continued*

Oven:

Roasting oven

Prepare in advance:

The kebabs can be made and kept in the fridge for up to 2 hours

Freeze:

Yes, uncooked

4   When you are ready to cook the kebabs, baste with the marinade then hang the dish from the top set of runners in the roasting oven for 10 minutes.

5   Remove from the oven, turn the skewers over and return to the oven for a further 5 minutes to finish cooking.

6   Serve at once, scattered with chopped coriander.

salmon and asparagus with cheat's hollandaise

Serves 4

4 salmon steaks

1 bunch, about 8 oz (225g) fresh English asparagus

2 egg yolks

4 oz (110g) butter

1 tbsp lemon juice

Salt and pepper

Oven:

Roasting oven, 200C, 400F, Gas 6

Prepare in advance:

Keep the uncooked fish and asparagus in the fridge for up to 12 hours

Prepare ahead:

Keep warm in the simmering or warming oven for up to half an hour, but do not make the sauce until the last minute!

Freeze:

Not this one! Particularly not the sauce, which will separate into rich savoury scrambled egg.

1   Line a small roasting tin with Bake-O-Glide.

2   Lay the salmon steaks and asparagus in the tin, then cover with foil. Hang the tin from the third set of runners for 12–15 minutes until the fish is cooked and the asparagus is tender.

3   *For the sauce*: Put the yolks into a bowl. Heat the butter in a pan on the simmering plate until boiling, then whisk the yolks and pour the butter onto them, whisking all the time. When all the butter has been incorporated and emulsified, season with salt, pepper and lemon juice.

4   Put the cooked salmon onto plates, pour over the sauce and top each with a few spears of asparagus. Summer on a plate!

monkfish and
bacon roll

Serves 4 – 5

1lb (450g) monkfish tail fillet (or cod loin fillet)

10–12 rashers streaky bacon

1 tbsp chopped fresh lemon thyme

Salt and pepper

To serve:

1 large swede

1 celeriac root

1 pack (150g) Boursin garlic cheese

Oven:

Roasting oven, 200C, 400F, Gas 6

Prepare in advance:

Keep uncooked fish in the fridge for up to 12 hours

Prepare ahead:

Keep the cooked fish and mash separate in the simmering or warming oven for up to 1 hour, but lay the fish onto the mash just before serving in case the fishy juices make the mash watery

Freeze:

Uncooked fish only, defrost then cook from number 5

1   Put the pack of Boursin onto the back of the Aga to soften.

2   Peel the swede and celeriac. Cut into even sized pieces and put into a pan of cold water. Bring to the boil then drain off all the water, cover with a lid and put into the simmering oven for 20 minutes until soft. Drain off any excess water given off during cooking, then tip in the warm cheese and mash well.

3   Meanwhile, cut the fish in half lengthways, remove the bone and lay on a board, top to tail, to make a long round sausage shape.

4   Stretch the bacon rashers and lay on a board in a rectangle. Scatter with the thyme then set the fish onto the bacon then bring up each rasher and wrap around the fish in a plait.

5   Line a large roasting tin with Bake-O-Glide and set the fish parcel into the tin. Hang from the second set of runners in the roasting oven for about 15 minutes, until the bacon is browned and crisp. Remove from the oven and allow to rest.

6   Spoon the celeriac mash onto a plate and lay the cooked fish on top of it.

ish

sole with leeks and pesto

Serves 4

2 Dover soles

2 medium leeks

1 oz (25g) butter

Salt and pepper

For the pesto:

1 tbsp pine nuts

2 cloves garlic

Handful basil leaves

Grated rind of a lemon

2 anchovy fillets

½ oz (15g) grated parmesan cheese

4 tbsp olive oil

Oven:

Roasting oven, 200C, 400F, Gas 6

Prepare in advance:

Make the pesto up to 3 days in advance. Prepare the fish and leeks, cover and keep in the fridge for up to 24 hours

Prepare ahead:

The fish will keep warm in the simmering oven for up to half an hour

Freeze:

The pesto yes, the complete dish no, as the fish tends to wilt on reheating.

If sole is too extravagant, try with rolled fillets of plaice.

1 First make the pesto: Put all the ingredients except the oil into a processor and whizz, or grind in a pestle and mortar, to a mush. Add the oil a little at a time, until it has thickened and emulsified.

2 Set the butter in a bowl on the back of the Aga to melt. Trim the leeks, then slice them thinly.

3 Skin the dark top of the fish and loosen the fillets (or get the fishmonger to do this for you!). Open out the fillets and spread generously with the pesto. Close the fish up again over the pesto.

4 Line the large roasting tin with Bake-O-Glide and scatter the leek slices into the tin. Pour over the melted butter and stir to coat the leeks with the butter.

5 Lay the soles onto the buttery leeks and cover the whole tin with foil.

6 Hang the tin from the third set of runners in the roasting oven and cook for 12–15 minutes, until the fish is cooked through.

7 Trim the frilly bits off the edges of the fish if you like, then lift the fish, scooping up the leeks below, onto a serving dish.

8 Serve with a squeeze of lemon juice over the top.

aga baked rice
with salmon

Serves 4 – 6

3 salmon fillet pieces

1 lemon

1 onion

1 clove garlic

2 tbsp olive oil

½ pint (225g) easy-cook rice

Pinch saffron

¾ pint (450ml) stock or water or water-mixed-with wine

Salt and pepper

2 tbsp chopped fresh dill

Optional prawns, mixed shellfish, etc.

Oven:

Simmering oven,

130C, 250F, Gas 1

Prepare in advance:

Cooked, cooled rice will keep in the fridge for up to 24 hours

Prepare ahead:

Will keep warm for up to an hour in simmering or warming oven

Freeze:

Don't see why not!

1   Cut the salmon fillet into ½" (1cm) cubes.

2   Grate the rind of the lemon and mix with the salmon. Squeeze the juice of the lemon. Set aside until needed.

3   Peel and chop the onion, crush the garlic.

4   Heat the oil in a large pan on the simmering plate, add onion and garlic and cook until sizzling, then cover and put into the simmering oven for about 15 minutes to soften.

5   Stir the rice and saffron into the onions, then pour over the stock. Season, stir and bring to the boil on the boiling plate. Cover and put into the simmering oven for about 15 minutes.

6   Add the salmon and lemon mixture (with some optional prawns, mixed shellfish etc) and cook for a further 5 minutes. Just before serving, stir in the lemon juice and dill.

creamy
fish pie

Serves 4 – 5

1 lb (450g) potatoes

1/4 pint (150ml) milk

1 oz (25g) butter

Salt and pepper

1 1/2 lb (600g) white fish – cod, haddock, etc

14 oz (400g) tub crème fraîche

1 tbsp Dijon mustard

Salt and pepper

Oven:

Simmering oven, 130C, 250F, Gas 1 and roasting oven, 200C, 400F, Gas 6

Prepare in advance:

Keep the prepared pie in the fridge for up to 24 hours before cooking

Prepare ahead:

Keep warm in the simmering or warming oven for up to an hour

Freeze:

Yes, defrost and reheat in the roasting oven for about 25 minutes

1 For the topping: Put the milk and butter in a mug and set on the back of the Aga to warm up. Cut the potatoes into even sized pieces and put into a pan. Cover with water and bring to the boil. Once they have boiled hard for a minute, drain, cover and put into the simmering oven for 35–45 minutes until soft.

2 Pour the hot, buttery milk onto the cooked potatoes and mash together, seasoning generously. Set aside to cool for a few minutes.

3 For the base of the pie: Cut the fish into 2" (5cms) pieces and put into a wide ovenproof dish. Mix the crème fraîche with the mustard and seasoning, then pour over the fish.

4 Pile the potato onto the fish and make pretty patterns with a fork (or pipe it on if you are feeling really keen).

5 Set the grid shelf on the lowest set of runners and put the pie onto the shelf and cook for 35–40 minutes until golden brown.

hot prawn and mango stir fry

Serves 4

20 peeled raw king prawns - about 9 oz (250g)

Bunch spring onions

1" (2½ cms) piece root ginger

1 clove garlic

1 small red chilli

1 mango

2 tsp sun dried tomato purée

1 tbsp dark soy sauce

2 tbsp rice vinegar

½ tsp sesame oil

2 tbsp groundnut oil

Salt and pepper

Oven:

Roasting oven to heat the pan, then boiling plate

Prepare in advance:

Chop all the ingredients and keep in the fridge for up to 12 hours before cooking

Prepare ahead:

No, this is a cook and go meal!

Freeze:

No

1 Put a large, wide based heavy pan or wok into the roasting oven to heat up before you start preparing the stir fry.

2 Rinse and trim the spring onions, then slice thinly. Peel and grate the ginger and garlic. Halve the chilli and remove the seeds, then chop finely. Mix together the onions, garlic, ginger and chilli.

3 Peel the mangoes and remove the flesh. Cut into ½" (1cm) chunks.

4 Mix together the tomato purée, soy sauce, rice vinegar and sesame oil (in a jam jar is easiest).

5 Transfer the hot pan to the boiling plate and add the groundnut oil. Tip in the spring onion mixture and stir fry for a minute. Add the prawns and continue to stir fry for another minute, then tip in the mango pieces. Stir again, then finally pour in the soy sauce mixture and stir until boiling.

6 Tip the hot prawn mixture onto a plate of rice and eat at once.

roasting a joint

Take a joint of meat – leg of lamb, topside of beef, leg of pork, capon, chicken etc. Wipe the joint with kitchen paper to dry.

Rub pork skin with salt for extra crispy crackling. Rub capon or chicken skin with salt, pepper and tarragon, cut up an onion and a lemon and push into the cavity. Rub mustard onto a beef joint. Make cuts in a lamb joint and push slivers of garlic and sprigs of rosemary into the meat.

Fast roasting

Line the roasting tin with Bake-O-Glide and put in the meat. Hang the tin from the third set of runners in the roasting oven and cook – 12 min per lb for beef, 20 min per lb for lamb and chicken, 25 min per lb for pork.

Medium roasting

Put the meat into the roasting oven for one third of the cooking time, to allow the joint to seal and brown, then move to the simmering oven, for the entire minutes per pound cooking time.

When cooked, remove the meat and allow to rest for at least 10 minutes to allow the juices to settle, whilst you make the gravy.

gravy

Making the gravy is often the most stressful part of cooking Sunday lunch, you stand there stirring the gravy on the heat, waiting for someone to come and lay the table for lunch or giving up and laying it yourself, while the gravy burns and goes lumpy. No longer . . . cooking the gravy on the floor of the oven leaves you free to get completely sorted before serving up the meal, with no stress at all!

1   Pour off all but 2 tbsp of the fat from the tin.

2   Stir in 2 tbsp flour, then blend in a pint (550ml) of stock – maybe adding a spoonful of wine – and for lamb a teaspoonful of redcurrant jelly, for beef a teaspoonful of Dijon mustard, for chicken some tarragon.

3   Stir well then put the tin onto the floor of the roasting oven for 5 minutes.

4   Stir and return to the oven for 5 more minutes and the gravy will be boiling and thickened, ready to stir and serve.

lamb and walnut tagine

Serves 4

4 lamb shanks

2 onions

1 tsp ground ginger

1 tsp ground cinnamon

1 tsp ground cumin

1 orange

1 tsp caster sugar

1 pint (450ml) stock

10 semi dried figs

2 oz (55g) walnut halves

Salt and pepper

Oven:

Roasting oven, 200C, 400F, Gas 6, then

simmering oven, 130C, 250F, Gas 1

Prepare in advance:

Cook the tagine a day in advance, chill overnight and skim any fat off the top before bringing to the boil in the roasting oven for 20 minutes and transferring to the simmering oven until you are ready to eat.

Prepare ahead:

Keep the tagine warm in the simmering or warming oven for an extra hour

Freeze:

Yes. Defrost and reheat in the roasting oven for 25 minutes

1   Season the lamb shanks with salt and pepper, then set them onto the grill rack in the large roasting tin, over a piece of Bake-O-Glide. Hang from the second set of runners in the roasting oven and cook for 20 minutes, until starting to brown and the fat is running.

2   Peel and slice the onion. Heat the oil in a large heavy based casserole on the simmering plate and add the onion. Cook until sizzling, then cover and put into the simmering oven for 15 minutes to soften.

3   Remove the lamb from the roasting oven and the onions from the simmering oven.

4   Cut the peel from the orange into strips with a peeler. Stir the spices into the onions, add the orange peel, sugar and lamb shanks. Pour over the stock and bring to the boil on the boiling plate. When boiling, cover and transfer to the simmering oven for 3 hours.

5   Remove from the oven, add the figs and walnuts then return to the simmering oven to cook for a further 30 minutes. Serve with couscous or Aga rice.

lamb steaks with minty sauce

Serves 4

4 lamb leg steaks

1 tbsp olive oil

¼ pint (150ml) red wine

2 tbsp mint jelly

2 cloves garlic

Salt and pepper

Oven:

Roasting oven, 200C, 400F, Gas 6

Prepare in advance:

No need, just sling it all together at the last minute

Prepare ahead:

Keep warm in the simmering oven or warming oven for up to 30 minutes

Freeze:

Yes, defrost and reheat in the roasting oven for 20 minutes

This works well with venison steaks, using cranberry sauce instead of the mint jelly.

1   Heat a large sauté pan in the roasting oven for 5 minutes. Transfer the pan to the boiling plate.

2   Heat the olive oil in the pan, then lay in the steaks. Put the pan onto the floor of the roasting oven for 5 minutes, then take out and turn the steaks over. Return to the oven for a further 3–5 minutes. Remove the steaks from the pan and leave to rest on a plate in the simmering oven.

3   Crush the garlic and add to the meat juices in the pan, together with the wine and mint jelly. Bring to the boil on the simmering plate, then return the pan to the floor of the roasting oven for 5 minutes, to boil and reduce.

4   Serve the sauce poured over the steaks.

Cooking the steaks on a very hot pan on the floor of the roasting oven ensures a well-sealed and crisp outer with tender pink meat inside.

braised lamb
bretonne

Serves 4 – 6

3½ – 4 lbs (2kg) leg lamb

8 oz (225g) tomatoes

1 clove garlic

Salt and pepper

1 tbsp olive oil

3 fl oz (100ml) stock

3 fl oz (100ml) white wine

1 bayleaf

Salt and pepper

Oven:

Simmering oven,

130C, 250F, Gas 1

Prepare in advance:

Cook the casserole a day in advance, chill overnight and skim any fat off the top before bringing to the boil in the roasting oven for 20 minutes and transferring to the simmering oven until you are ready to eat.

Prepare ahead:

Keep warm in the simmering or warming oven for an extra hour

Freeze:

Yes, defrost and reheat in the roasting oven for 25 minutes

1 Scald and skin the tomatoes, remove the seeds and chop the flesh – or just chop the tomatoes up a bit.

2 Heat the oil in a large casserole and add the lamb. Fry on the floor of the roasting oven, shaking the pan once or twice until it is brown all over. Tip in the tomatoes and crush in the garlic, season and pour over the stock and wine, add the bayleaf and bring to the boil.

3 When boiling well, cover and place in the simmering oven for 2 hours.

4 Check the sauce before serving – it may need a couple of spoons of water or stock if too thick.

5 Serve with haricot beans.

rack of lamb
with lavender

Serves 4

2 racks of lamb, trimmed

1 medium onion

2 tbsp fresh lavender flowers

1 tbsp balsamic vinegar

2 tbsp olive oil

1 lemon

Salt and pepper

Oven:

Roasting oven, 200C, 400F, Gas 6

Prepare in advance:

Keep the bag of marinating lamb
in the fridge for up to 24 hours

Prepare ahead:

Keep warm in the simmering oven
or warming oven for half an hour

Freeze:

*In the marinade, yes. Defrost and
cook from no. 3*

*This is very quick and easy, especially
if you can get the butcher to trim the
racks of lamb for you!*

1   Trim the racks of lamb of all their fat, so the bones
show. Cut each into two pieces of about 3 cutlets
each. Put into a heavy duty plastic bag.

2   Grate the rind of the lemon and squeeze the juice,
peel and chop the onion and garlic. Mix together the
lemon rind and juice, garlic, onion, oil, seasoning and
lavender flowers. Pour this marinade into the bag
and seal tightly. Shake to coat the meat and leave to
marinate for at least an hour, or overnight.

3   When ready to cook, line a small roasting tin with
Bake-O-Glide and tip in the meat, reserving the
juices. Hang the tin from the second set of runners
and roast for about 15 minutes, then pour over the
rest of the marinade and put the tin on the floor of the
roasting oven for 5 minutes to boil and reduce the
juices.

4   Remove the meat from the tin and allow to rest for 5
minutes before carving into separate cutlets. Serve
with the sauce poured over.

turkish lamb pilaf

Serves 4 – 5

1 tbsp (15g) pine nuts

1 tbsp (15g) slivered almonds

1lb (450g) lamb neck fillet

1 onion

1 clove garlic

1/2 tsp ground cinnamon

2 tbsp olive oil

1/2 pint (275ml) rice

3/4 pint (425ml) stock or water or water-mixed-with wine

4 oz (110g) ready to eat dried apricots, sliced

Salt and pepper

1 tbsp chopped fresh mint

Oven:

Floor of roasting oven, then simmering oven, 130C, 250F, Gas 1

Prepare in advance:

The cooked, cooled pilaf will keep in the fridge for up to 24 hours, cover and reheat in the roasting oven for 20 minutes

Prepare ahead:

Will keep warm in simmering or warming oven for up to an hour

Freeze:

Don't see why not! Defrost, cover and reheat in the roasting oven for 25 minutes

1 Put the pine nuts and almonds into a large pan and cook on the boiling plate for a minute or two until toasted. Set them aside.

2 Chop the apricots. Cut the lamb into 1/2" (1cm) cubes. Peel and chop the onion, crush the garlic.

3 Heat the oil in the pan and add onion, garlic, cinnamon and lamb. Cook on the boiling plate for a minute, until sizzling. Stir, then put onto the floor of the roasting oven for a further 10 minutes to brown.

4 Transfer the pan to the boiling plate, stir in the rice and apricots, and pour on the stock. Season, stir well and bring to the boil. Cover and put in the simmering oven for 15–20 minutes.

5 Just before serving, stir in the chopped mint.

rich venison casserole

Serves 6

1½ lb (750g) diced venison

1 tbsp olive oil

1 oz (25g) butter

1 onion

1 clove garlic

½ pint (275ml) good stock

1 tbsp plain flour

1 tsp cocoa powder

8 oz (250g) prepared chestnuts

4 oz (110g) chestnut mushrooms

Sprig of fresh thyme

Salt and pepper

Oven:

Simmering oven,
130C, 250F, Gas 1

Prepare in advance:

Keep the cooked, cooled
casserole in the fridge for up to 24
hours

Prepare ahead:

Keep the casserole in the
simmering or warming oven for an
additional hour or so until you are
ready to eat.

Freeze:

*Yes, defrost then reheat in the
roasting oven for 25 minutes*

1   Melt the butter and oil together in a large, heavy pan
on the boiling plate. Tip in the venison and once
sizzling, transfer to the floor of the roasting oven to
brown.

2   Whilst it is browning, slice the onion and crush the
garlic. Quarter the mushrooms if large, or halve them
if small.

3   Remove the pan of venison from the oven, shake it to
turn the meat over and add the onion and garlic. Stir,
then return to the floor of the roasting oven to
continue browning for 5 minutes.

4   Put the pan onto the boiling plate and stir in the
chestnuts, flour, cocoa, thyme and seasoning. Slowly
blend in the stock and stir until boiling. Cover and
transfer to the simmering oven for 1½ to 2 hours.

5   About half an hour before you want to eat it, take the
casserole from the oven, stir in the mushrooms then
put it back into the simmering oven.

6   Serve with creamy mashed potatoes.

osso bucco

Serves 4 – 5

2 lb (900g) veal shin

2 tbsp olive oil

1 onion

1 clove garlic

¼ pint (150ml) light stock

1 orange

½ tbsp cornflour

2 tomatoes

Salt and pepper

Oven:

Simmering oven,

130C, 250F, Gas 1

Prepare in advance:

Keep the cooked, cooled
casserole in the fridge for up to 24
hours

Prepare ahead:

Keep the casserole in the
simmering or warming oven for an
additional hour until you are ready
to eat

Freeze:

*Yes, defrost then reheat in the
roasting oven for 25 minutes*

1   Heat the oil in a large, heavy pan on the boiling plate.
    Add the pieces of veal and, once sizzling, transfer to
    the floor of the roasting oven to brown.

2   Whilst the veal is browning, slice the onion and crush
    the garlic. Peel the skin of the orange with a peeler
    and squeeze the juice. Mix the juice with the
    cornflour. Slice the rind into shreds.

3   Remove the veal from the oven and turn the meat
    over. Add the onion and garlic. Stir then return to the
    floor of the roasting oven to continue browning for 5
    minutes.

4   Take the pan of browned meat and onions from the
    oven, stir in the orange juice/cornflour mixture,
    orange rind, stock and seasoning. Bring to the boil
    on the boiling plate, stirring all the time. Cover and
    put into the simmering oven for 2 hours.

5   Put the tomatoes into a bowl and pour a kettle of
    boiling water over them, leave for a minute then slip
    the skins off. Cut into quarters and remove the pips,
    then slice. (*Or just cut the tomatoes into pieces!*)

6   When the veal is cooked, remove from the oven, stir
    in the tomatoes and check the seasoning. Put the
    pan, uncovered, onto the floor of the roasting oven for
    5–10 minutes to reduce the sauce, and serve with
    mashed potato, rice or creamy polenta.

guinea fowl and sloe stew

Serves 4

4 guinea fowl breasts (or pheasant)

1 medium onion

2 cloves garlic

1 tbsp plain flour

1 tbsp olive oil

½ oz (15g) butter

½ pint (275ml) pheasant stock

4 tbsp sloe gin

1 tsp chopped rosemary

Salt and pepper

Oven:

Simmering oven,

130C, 250F, Gas 1

Prepare in advance:

Keep the cooked, cooled stew in the fridge for up to 24 hours

Prepare ahead:

Keep warm in the simmering or warming oven for half an hour

Freeze:

Yes, defrost and reheat in the roasting oven for 25 minutes

A very autumnal dish, warm and comforting.

1 Melt the butter and oil in a heavy pan on the simmering plate.

2 Cut the breasts into 2" (5cms) chunks, peel and slice the onion, crush the garlic.

3 Transfer the pan to the boiling plate and add the meat and vegetables. Stir-fry for 5 minutes until browned. Add the flour and rosemary, stirring, and then pour in the stock and sloe gin.

4 Bring to the boil, then cover and cook in the simmering oven for 25–30 minutes until tender.

5 Serve with celeriac and potato mash and a green vegetable.

duck with sour cherries

Serves 4

  4 duck breasts

  1 tbsp olive oil

  1 small onion

  1 clove garlic

  3 oz (75g) dried sour cherries

  3 tbsp port

  3 fl oz (100ml) stock

  Salt and pepper

Oven:

  Roasting oven, 200C, 400F, Gas 6

Prepare in advance:

  Make the sauce and keep in the fridge for up to 24 hours

Prepare ahead:

  Keep warm in the simmering or warming oven for half an hour

Freeze:

  No

Removing the skin from the duck more than halves the calories and fat in this dish at a stroke! Put the duck skins into the small roasting tin in the simmering oven for an hour. The fat will run off, to be strained and kept in a jar in the fridge for wonderful roast potatoes or fried bread.

1 Put a ridged grill pan or wide sauté pan into the roasting oven to heat up for 5 minutes (or 10 minutes if cast iron).

2 Put the cherries and port into a small pan and heat gently on the simmering plate for a couple of minutes. Draw off the heat and allow to stand for 15 minutes to allow the cherries to absorb the wine. Chop the onion and crush the garlic.

3 Remove the skins from the duck and rub the fat side of the duck skins over the inside of the pan. If it sizzles, the pan is hot enough to grill the meat. Cook the breasts in the hot pan on the floor of the roasting oven for 5–10 minutes, turning once. When they are cooked, remove to rest in the simmering oven while you make the sauce.

4 Add the onion and garlic to the pan and stir together on the simmering plate. When sizzling, tip in the stock, prepared cherries and seasoning. Transfer to the floor of the roasting oven for 3 minutes to boil and reduce.

5 Serve the duck breasts carved into thick slices, with the sauce poured over.

thai coconut chicken

Serves 4

4 chicken breasts

2 tbsp groundnut oil

1 bunch spring onions

1 clove garlic

1 tin (400ml) coconut milk

4 Thai lime leaves

2 tbsp Thai fish sauce

1 tbsp Thai red curry paste

1/4 pint (150ml) stock

1 tbsp chopped fresh coriander

8 oz (225g) rice

1/4 pint (150ml) water

Oven:

Floor of roasting oven and
simmering oven,
130C, 250F, Gas 1

Prepare in advance:

Prepare and chop all the
ingredients and keep in the fridge
for up to 24 hours before cooking

Prepare ahead:

Keep warm in the simmering oven
or warming oven for up to an hour

Freeze:

*Not this one, the chicken goes
stringy when reheated!*

1 Put the rice into a saucepan. Add 1/2 pint (300ml) coconut milk and the water. Bring to the boil, cover and put into the simmering oven.

2 Peel and crush the garlic; trim and slice the spring onions, slice the chicken breasts.

3 Heat the oil in a deep frying pan or casserole. Add the chicken breasts and fry – on the floor of the roasting oven – for 10 minutes, turning once.

4 Transfer the pan to the boiling plate. Add the onions, garlic, the rest of the coconut milk and all the remaining ingredients to the pan, stir together and bring to the boil, then cover and put into the simmering oven for 15 minutes until cooked through.

5 Serve the chicken on top of the rice, with the sauce poured over and a scattering of chopped fresh coriander leaves.

The coconut-flavoured rice is very rich on its own, but it adds an unusual depth of flavour to the dish.

pink turkey casserole

Serves 4 – 5

1½ lbs (750g) turkey meat

1 tbsp olive oil

1 onion

1 clove garlic

1 tbsp plain flour

6 tomatoes

¼ pint (150ml) stock/red wine mixed

½ tsp smoked paprika

¼ pint (142ml tub) soured cream

2 tbsp chopped chives

Salt and pepper

Oven:

Simmering oven,
130C, 250F, Gas 1

Prepare in advance:

Keep the cooked and cooled casserole in the fridge for up to 24 hours

Prepare ahead:

Keep the casserole warm in the simmering or warming oven for up to an hour

Freeze:

Yes, defrost and reheat in the roasting oven for 25 minutes

1 Cut the meat into 2" (5cms) chunks. Heat the oil in a pan on the simmering plate, and fry the meat until browned – on the floor of the roasting oven – turning occasionally.

2 Slice the onion and crush the garlic. Add to the pan, cover and transfer to the simmering oven for 5 minutes for the onion to soften.

3 Stir in the flour and paprika and then add the stock/red wine, stirring until blended. Roughly chop the tomatoes and add to the pan. Season and bring to the boil.

4 Cover and cook in the simmering oven for 30–40 minutes, then stir in the soured cream, sprinkle with chopped chives and serve.

This was created for one of the Aga 'Think Pink' breast cancer awareness campaign demonstrations, where every dish should be pink – not easy without resorting to cochineal!

lapsang
chicken

Serves 4

4 chicken breasts

4 slices (70g) Black Forest ham

1 ball preserved stem ginger

1/2 pint (275ml) Lapsang Suchong tea – made and strained

Rind and juice of a lemon

Salt and pepper

1 tsp cornflour

1 tbsp chopped parsley

Oven:

Roasting oven,

200C, 400F, Gas 6

Prepare in advance:

Wrap the prepared chicken in the ham and keep in the fridge for up to 24 hours.

Prepare ahead:

Keep warm in the simmering or warming oven for up to an hour

Freeze:

Yes, either cooked or uncooked and ready to go into the oven as soon as it defrosts

1 Remove the skin from the chicken breasts. Place between two sheets of cling film and beat with a rolling pin to flatten.

2 Grate the stem ginger and divide between the chicken breasts. Grate the lemon rind onto the meat. Lay a piece of ham onto each flattened breast then roll up, lengthways with the join underneath.

3 Line the small roasting tin with Bake-O-Glide. Lay the chicken pieces in the tin. Squeeze the lemon juice into the tea. Pour the tea over the chicken.

4 Cover with foil and hang the tin from the third set of runners in the roasting oven for about 20 minutes, until the meat is cooked through.

5 Remove the meat from the tin and put onto a serving plate.

6 Pour the juices into a bowl, add seasoning and cornflour and mix well. Return to the tin and place on the floor of the oven for 5 minutes, until thickened and slightly reduced. Pour the sauce over the chicken, scatter some chopped parsley on top and serve on a bed of rice.

spiked chicken

Serves 4

4 chicken breasts or 8 chicken thighs

2 tbsp olive oil

1 medium onion

1 clove garlic

8 peppadew peppers

1 tin (400g) chopped tomatoes

1 sprig thyme

Oven:

Floor of roasting oven then simmering oven, 130C, 250F, Gas 1

Prepare in advance:

Keep the cooked, cooled casserole in the fridge for up to 24 hours, reheat in the roasting oven for 25 minutes

Prepare ahead:

Keep warm in the warming oven or simmering oven for up to 45 minutes

Freeze:

Yes, defrost then reheat in the roasting oven for 25 minutes. Chicken thighs are much more forgiving to freeze then breasts, which tend to get a bit stringy as they defrost

1 Cut the meat into $1/2$" (1cm) slices. Peel and slice the onion and crush the garlic. Drain the peppers and slice them.

2 Heat the oil in a heavy pan on the boiling plate and add the chicken and onions. Stir over the heat until sizzling, then transfer to the floor of the roasting oven for 5–10 minutes to brown, shaking once or twice to turn the meat.

3 Tip in the garlic, peppers, tomatoes and thyme leaves. Bring to the boil then cover and put into the simmering oven for 15 minutes.

4 Serve with rice.

Peppadew peppers are small, red, sweet, South African peppers that come in a jar. They have just a hint of a bite, not quite chillies but nearly!

spicy moroccan lemon chicken

Serves 4

4 chicken breasts or 8 chicken thighs

2 tbsp olive oil

1 medium onion

1 clove garlic

2 tbsp harissa paste

2 preserved lemons

$1/4$ pint (150ml) stock

Handful fresh parsley, chopped

Freeze:

Yes, defrost then reheat in the roasting oven for 25 minutes

1 If using chicken breasts, cut the meat into $1/2$" (1cm) slices. If using chicken thighs, leave whole. Peel and slice the onion and crush the garlic. Drain the lemons and slice.

2 Heat the oil in a heavy pan on the boiling plate and

spicy moroccan lemon chicken *continued*

Oven:

Floor of roasting oven then simmering oven, 130C, 250F, Gas 1

Prepare in advance:

Keep the cooked, cooled casserole in the fridge for up to 24 hours, reheat in the roasting oven for 25 minutes

Prepare ahead:

Keep warm in the warming oven or simmering oven for up to 45 minutes

add the chicken and onions. Stir over the heat until sizzling, then transfer to the floor of the roasting oven for 10 minutes to brown, shaking once or twice to turn the meat.

3   Tip in the garlic, lemons, harissa and stock. Bring to the boil then cover and put into the simmering oven for 15 minutes. (If you prefer a more reduced sauce, boil, uncovered, on the floor of the roasting oven for 5-7 minutes.)

4 Scatter over the parsley and serve with couscous.

Frying the meat on the floor of the roasting oven reduces cooking smells and you don't have to wipe up the fat that gets spattered from the pan.

chicken with lavender and honey

Serves 4

4 chicken breasts

1 tbsp dried lavender flowers

1 tbsp runny honey

2 oranges

2 tbsp olive oil

1 clove garlic

Oven:

Roasting oven, 400F, 200C, Gas 6

Prepare in advance:

Keep the chicken in the marinade in the fridge for up to 24 hours

Prepare ahead:

Keep the chicken warm in the simmering oven or warming oven for up to 45 minutes

Freeze:

Yes, uncooked in the marinade

1   Put the chicken breasts into a roasting bag. Add the lavender flowers, honey, grated rind and juice of the oranges, crushed garlic and olive oil. Seal the bag and shake well to mix. Leave to marinate for an hour or more.

2   When ready to cook, snip the top of the bag to allow the air to expand, then put it into a roasting tin lined with Bake-O-Glide and hang from the third set of runners for about 20 minutes.

3   Serve the chicken with the sauce poured over.

This unusual dish came about when I was asked by a local flower club to demonstrate cooking with flowers! If you prefer not to use lavender, try fresh rosemary, which also has a strong flavour.

stir-fried
chicken satay

Serves 4

6 boneless chicken thigh joints

1 red chilli

1" (2cm) piece ginger

1 clove garlic

2 tbsp (30ml) crunchy peanut butter

2 tbsp chopped fresh coriander

1 tsp caster sugar

4 spring onions

2 tbsp rice vinegar

3 tbsp groundnut oil

1 tbsp Thai fish sauce

Oven:

Boiling plate

Prepare in advance:

24 hours in the marinade

Prepare ahead:

Keep warm for up to 30 minutes in the warming oven

Freeze:

Yes, in the marinade

1 Cut the chicken meat into thin strips and put into a heavy duty plastic bag.

2 Halve the chilli, remove the seeds and the white membrane (this is the hottest part!) and put into a small processor with the peeled garlic and ginger. Chop finely. Add the rice vinegar, coriander, sugar, oil, trimmed spring onions, peanut butter and fish sauce and process briefly to mix. Tip into the plastic bag and seal, then shake to coat the meat in the marinade.

3 Leave to marinate for at least an hour, or overnight.

4 Put a wok or deep, heavy frying pan into the roasting oven to heat up – cast iron takes up to 10 minutes, aluminium about 5 minutes.

5 Transfer the hot pan to the boiling plate and tip in the contents of the bag.

6 Stir-fry for about 5 minutes, then serve on a bed of rice.

You can stir-fry in a deep frying pan, cast iron casserole or wok, whatever comes to hand! The secret is to get the pan as hot as possible before putting it onto the boiling plate to cook.

boston baked beans with bacon

Serves 4 – 6

- 1 lb (450g) haricot beans
- 1 oz (25g) dark muscovado sugar
- 4 tbsp black treacle
- 1 tsp salt
- 1 tsp dry mustard powder
- 1 tsp ground allspice
- 2 medium onions
- 1 tbsp olive oil
- 2 lb (900g) gammon joint
- 2 tbsp dark rum

Oven:

Simmering oven,
130C, 250F, Gas 1

Prepare in advance:

Keep the cooked, cooled casserole in the fridge for up to 24 hours, the flavours mellow together wonderfully

Prepare ahead:

Leave the casserole in the simmering oven or warming oven for an extra hour

Freeze:

Yes, defrost and reheat in the roasting oven for 25 minutes

This seems to be very fashionable at the moment – it is so easy to make, just chuck it all together and leave in the simmering oven all afternoon!

1. Cover the beans with cold water and leave to soak overnight. Next day, drain the beans and put into a large pan with fresh water to cover by at least an inch (2½cms). Bring to the boil and boil hard for 15 minutes, then cover and transfer to the simmering oven for an hour. (*Alternatively, open a standard sized tin of haricot beans and continue*).

2. Peel and chop the onions. Heat the oil in a large casserole on the simmering plate and add the onions. When sizzling, cover and put into the simmering oven for 15 minutes to soften. Cut the piece of gammon into 2" (5cms) chunks.

3. Drain the beans, keeping the water this time, and put into the casserole. Add the sugar, treacle, salt, mustard and allspice. Stir together. Add the pieces of gammon. Pour over enough of the bean-cooking water to cover (you may need to add a little extra water) and bring to the boil.

4. Cover and transfer to the simmering oven for about 3 hours, then remove the lid and continue to cook for another hour until the meat is tender and the sauce reduced.

5. Stir in the rum just before serving.

pork with apricots
and leeks

Serves 4 – 5

1½ lbs (650g) pork fillet

1 tbsp walnut oil

2 medium leeks

3 oz (75g) ready to eat dried apricots

4 tbsp dry white vermouth

¼ pint (150ml) orange juice

¼ pint (150ml) stock

1 tbsp cornflour

Salt and pepper

Oven:

Simmering oven, 130C, 250F, Gas 1

Prepare in advance:

Keep the cooked, cooled casserole in the fridge for up to 24 hours

Prepare ahead:

Keep warm in the simmering oven or warming oven for up to an hour

Freeze:

Yes, defrost and reheat in the roasting oven for 25 minutes

The sweetness of the leeks and apricots make a lovely contrast with the very lean pork fillet.

1 Cut the pork fillet into ½" (1cm) slices.

2 Heat the oil in a large frying pan on the boiling plate and add the meat. Set onto the floor of the roasting oven to brown for 5 minutes, shaking occasionally to turn the meat.

3 Cut the leeks into thin slices and slice the apricots. Add the leeks and apricots, to the meat then return to the floor of the oven for another 2 minutes to brown.

4 Mix the cornflour with the orange juice. Tip the vermouth and stock into the pan of meat, leeks and apricot, then stir in the cornflour and orange juice mixture, stirring all the time. Season and bring to the boil, then cover and cook in the simmering oven for 20 minutes until tender.

5 Serve with rice and a green vegetable.

ginger pork
mystery stir fry

Serves 4 – 5

4 pork leg steaks

1 tbsp cornflour

½" (1cm) root ginger

5 spring onions

½ tsp Sichuan pepper

1 Put a wok, wide cast iron casserole or large frying pan into the roasting oven to heat up.

2 Cut the pork into very thin strips. Peel and crush the garlic and ginger, trim and slice the onions.

3 Mix the cornflour with 2 tbsp of cola and toss the pork strips in it.

ginger pork mystery stir fry *continued*

2 tbsp lemon juice

1 clove garlic

½ pint (275ml) Coca Cola or ginger beer

2 tbsp grapeseed oil

Oven:

Boiling plate

Prepare in advance:

Chop all the ingredients and keep them in the fridge for up to 12 hours before cooking

Prepare ahead:

No, this is instant food!

Freeze:

No

4   Put the hot pan onto the boiling plate and add the oil. Tip the pork into the pan and stir fry for a couple of minutes. Add the garlic, ginger and onions and stir fry for another minute or two. Pour on the cola, stirring.

5   Once it boils and thickens, serve at once on a bed of rice.

No one will ever guess the mystery ingredient in this stir fry – unless you confess or leave the can lying around! The 'secret' recipe for Coca Cola must contain a lot of ginger, as the flavours marry so well and the lemon juice cuts through any sweetness. If you prefer, substitute ginger beer for the coke.

pork with warm apples

Serves 4

4 pork steaks

2 Granny Smith apples

1 tbsp olive oil

2 tbsp lemon juice

1 tbsp runny honey

1 clove garlic, crushed

Salt and pepper

Oven:

Roasting oven, 200C, 400F, Gas 6

Prepare ahead:

24 hours uncooked

Freeze:

Yes

1   Core and quarter the apples, then cut each piece in half lengthways.

2   Mix together the oil, lemon juice, honey, garlic and seasoning. Add the apple pieces and stir.

3   Heat a wide, heavy based pan on the boiling plate for a couple of minutes, and add the pork steaks. Transfer to the floor of the roasting oven to fry for 5 minutes.

4   Remove the pan from the oven, turn the meat over and add the apple and marinade. Return to the floor of the oven for 10 minutes, until the meat is browned, the apple soft and the sauce reduced and thick.

5   Serve the pork steaks on a bed of mustardy mashed potato, with the apple pieces and sauce on top.

stuffed pork fillet
with orange sauce

Serves 6

2 pork fillets, each about 12 oz (350g)

10 rashers smoked streaky bacon

2 tbsp marmalade

Sauce:

1 medium onion

1 clove garlic

1 cooking apple

1 tbsp olive oil

2 tbsp marmalade

½ pint (275ml) orange juice

1 tbsp flour

Salt and pepper

Oven:

Roasting oven, 200C, 400F, Gas 6 and simmering oven, 130C, 250F, Gas 1

Prepare in advance:

Keep the prepared, uncooked meat and the cooked sauce in the fridge for up to 24 hours

Prepare ahead:

Keep warm in the simmering or warming oven for up to an hour

Freeze:

Yes, (meat uncooked, sauce cooked)

1 Cut a deep pocket into the fillets and smear the marmalade into the cuts. Lay the bacon onto a board and, with the back of a knife, stretch each rasher. Arrange 5 rashers together and lay one of the fillets, cut side up, onto the bacon.

2 Wrap the bacon around the fillet, alternating the rashers in a 'plait' and tuck the last end of the final rasher underneath. Repeat for the second fillet.

3 Line a small roasting tin with Bake-O-Glide and set the fillets into it. Hang from the third set of runners for about 20–30 minutes, until the bacon is crisp and browned.

4 For the sauce: Peel and chop the onion, garlic and apple. Melt the oil in a pan on the simmering plate and add the onion, garlic and apple. Heat until sizzling then cover and put into the simmering oven for 20 minutes to soften. When cooked, stir in the flour, orange juice and marmalade and bring to the boil. Liquidise the sauce, then return to the pan to keep warm.

5 To serve, carve the pork into ½" (1cm) slices and pour over a little sauce. Serve the rest of the sauce separately.

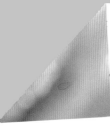

anny boogle's bacon kedgeree

Serves 4

8 oz (225g) long grain rice – half a pint in a measuring jug

³/₄ pint (425ml) water or light stock

4 eggs

¹/₂ lb (225g) streaky bacon

Salt and pepper

Oven:

Roasting oven, 200C, 400F, Gas 6 and simmering oven, 130C, 250F, Gas 1

Prepare in advance:

Not really, this a bit of a last minute thing

Prepare ahead:

Keep warm in the simmering oven or warming oven for up to half an hour

Freeze:

No the eggs go rubbery in the freezer!

1 Put the rice into a pan with the stock, stir, cover and bring to the boil on the boiling plate. Once boiling, transfer to the simmering oven for 15 minutes until the rice is cooked and has absorbed all the liquid.

2 Put the bacon onto the grill rack in the roasting tin and hang from the top set of runners in the roasting oven to grill for 10 minutes, until crisp. Remove from the oven and snip into small pieces with scissors.

3 Bring a pan of water to the boil and add the eggs, cover and simmer for 12 minutes then drain and cool under a cold running tap. Peel and chop the eggs.

4 Stir the cooked bacon and eggs into the rice, season and serve at once, with a salad or green peas.

8oz of rice will fill a ¹/₂ pint coffee mug, the water one and a half mugs.

If you use brown, black or red rice, or risotto rice, you will need to use 2 mugs of water to one of rice.

slow baked marmalade gammon

Serves 8 – 10

6 lb (3kg) gammon joint

¹/₂ tsp allspice berries

¹/₂ tsp cloves

¹/₂ tsp peppercorns

2–3 tbsp marmalade

2–3 tbsp demerara sugar to glaze

1 Soak the joint in cold water overnight. Line the large roasting tin with foil.

2 Grind the spices together and mix with the marmalade. Smear this all over the joint and lay it in the tin. Cover with foil and put into the simmering oven for about 40 minutes per pound, 80 minutes per kilo.

3 When the ham is cooked, remove from the oven,

slow baked marmalade gammon *continued*

Oven:

Simmering oven, 130C, 250F, Gas 1 and roasting oven, 200C, 400F, Gas 6

Prepare in advance:

Cook the gammon, cool, cover and keep in the fridge for up to 24 hours

Prepare ahead:

Keep the cooked, glazed gammon warm in the simmering or warming oven for up to an hour

Freeze:

Yes, defrost slowly!

open the package and peel away the skin. Score the fat then smear with a little more marmalade and the sugar. Bake in the roasting oven for 20 minutes until browned and glazed.

4 Serve, either hot with Hampshire sauce (see next recipe), or chilled with salad and mustard mayonnaise.

hampshire sauce

Serves 8 – 10

1 jar (340g) crab apple jelly

1 lemon

1 tbsp Dijon mustard

1/2 medium onion

1/4 pint (150ml) sweet sherry

1 tsp arrowroot

Oven:

Simmering plate

Prepare ahead:

Keep the cooled sauce in a jar in the fridge for up to 4 days

Freeze: *No*

1 Tip the contents of the jar into a pan.

2 Peel the onion and grate it with a very fine grater, or whizz in a processor.

3 Grate the rind of the lemon and squeeze the juice. Mix together the sherry, mustard and arrowroot, then stir into the pan, together with the lemon juice, rind and onion.

4 Set onto the simmering plate and gently bring to the boil, stirring all the time – the jelly will melt and dissolve and the arrowroot will thicken the sauce.

5 Pour into a jug and serve.

ham
lasagne

Serves 4 – 5

1lb (450g) cooked ham

1 tbsp olive oil

1 medium onion

1 tin (340g) chopped tomatoes

$\frac{1}{2}$ tsp dried thyme

Salt and pepper

9 lasagne sheets

1 oz (25g) butter

1 oz (25g) plain flour

$\frac{1}{2}$ pint (225ml) milk

2 oz (55g) grated cheddar cheese

Salt and pepper

Oven:

Simmering oven, 130C, 250F, Gas 1 and roasting oven, 400F, 200C, Gas 6

Prepare in advance:

Keep the prepared lasagne in the fridge for up to 24 hours before cooking

Prepare ahead:

Keep warm in the simmering oven or warming oven for up to an hour

Freeze:

Yes, defrost and reheat in the roasting oven for 25 minutes

A useful way to finish up leftovers from a ham joint.

1 Peel and chop the onion. Heat the oil in a pan on the simmering plate and add the onion. Stir until sizzling, then cover and put into the simmering oven for 15 minutes until the onion is softened. Once cooked, stir in the chopped tomatoes, herbs and seasoning.

2 Put the ham into a processor and chop – not too finely or it turns to a mush! Add the ham to the cooked onions and mix together.

3 Put a third of this mixture into an oven proof dish, then lay on three sheets of lasagne. Repeat this layering process until all the sauce and pasta have been used up in three layers.

4 Melt the butter in a pan on the simmering plate and stir in the flour. Blend in the milk and stir until boiling. Season well then pour over the dish of lasagne. Scatter the cheese over and bake in the centre of the roasting oven for 25–30 minutes until golden and bubbling.

5 Serve with a big salad and some crusty bread.

steak and kidney pudding

Serves 4-6

1½ lb (750g) stewing steak

½ lb (225g) ox kidney

1 onion

½ pt (275ml) best bitter

Salt and pepper

Pastry:

4 oz (110g) beef suet

8 oz (225g) self raising flour

1 tbsp Worcester sauce

About ¼ pint (150ml) water

2 tbsp plain flour

Oven:

Simmering oven, 130C, 250F, Gas 1

Prepare in advance:

Assemble the pudding and keep in the fridge for up to 12 hours before cooking

Prepare ahead:

Can sit for up to 2 extra hours in the simmering or warming oven!

Freeze:

Not this one, the pastry is not nice when it defrosts

1   To make the pastry: sift the flour into a bowl and stir in the suet. Add cold water one tablespoon at a time, mixing until you have a dough.

2   Knead for 2 minutes until pliable, then roll out to approx 14" (35cm) round. Cut out a quarter-sized slice and line a 2pt (1 litre) pudding basin with the large section. Re-roll the remaining quarter into an 8" (20cm) round to make a lid for the pudding.

3   Cut the beef and kidney into 1" (2½cm) cubes. Chop the onion. Put the plain flour into a plastic bag with plenty of salt and pepper.

4   Toss the meat and onion in the bag, then turn into the lined pudding basin. Mix together the Worcester sauce and beer and pour this over the meat.

5   Moisten the rim of the pastry lining and lay on the lid, pinching together the edges. Cover with buttered, pleated greaseproof paper and pleated foil, tie tightly with string (or clip the lid onto the plastic bowl!).

6   Take a long piece of foil and fold lengthways into a long strip, which goes under the basin, to act as a handle. Fill a large saucepan with water to come about a quarter of the way up the sides of the bowl, lower the basin into the pan and bring to the boil.

7   Cover with a lid and boil for 15 minutes on the boiling plate before transferring to the simmering oven for 6 hours.

8   To serve, lift out the pudding and wrap the bowl in a white linen napkin (or a tea towel!) before bringing to the table.

beef with molasses

Serves 4 – 5

1½ lbs (675g) stewing beef

1 medium onion

1 clove garlic

1 tbsp olive oil

1 tbsp plain flour

1 tbsp black treacle

1 can (330ml) Coca Cola

1 tbsp chopped fresh rosemary

Salt and pepper

Oven:

Simmering oven, 130C, 250F, Gas 1

Prepare in advance:

Keep the cooked, cooled stew in the fridge for up to 24 hours

Prepare ahead:

Keep warm in the simmering or warming oven for half an hour

Freeze:

Yes, defrost and reheat in the roasting oven for 25 minutes

1 Cut the beef into 1" (2cms) cubes. Chop the onion and crush the garlic.

2 Heat the oil in a casserole on the simmering plate. When hot, add the meat, onion and garlic. Stir until sizzling, then transfer to the floor of the roasting oven to brown for 5 minutes, shaking the pan occasionally to turn the meat.

3 When the meat has browned, stir in the flour, then the treacle and Coke. Add the herbs and seasoning and bring to the boil on the boiling plate, stirring all the time.

4 Once the casserole is boiling, cover with a tight fitting lid and put into the simmering oven for 2 hours.

5 Serve with rice or mashed potatoes and a green vegetable.

If you are using dried herbs instead of fresh, rub between your palms or grind through a mill to release the oil and flavour of the herbs.

thai beef salad

Serves 4

3 sirloin steaks

Bunch spring onions

½ cucumber

½ head Chinese leaves

2 stalks lemon grass

1 red chilli

1 lime

Dressing:

2 tbsp Thai fish sauce

Freeze: *No*

1 Put a cast iron or removable-handle griddle pan into the roasting oven to heat up.

2 Transfer the pan to the boiling plate and rub the fat side of the steaks over the ridges. Cook the steaks in the griddle pan on the boiling plate for about 5 minutes each side, turning only once, until medium rare. Remove from the pan and allow to rest and cool for 10–15 minutes.

3 Trim and slice the spring onions, cut the cucumber into matchstick-sized pieces, shred the Chinese

thai beef salad *continued*

2 tbsp grapeseed oil

1 tsp sesame oil

Salt and pepper

Oven:

Boiling plate

Prepare in advance:

Cook meat, prepare vegetables
but do not mix until just before
serving

leaves and chop the lemon grass and chilli finely.
Grate the rind of the lime and squeeze the juice.

4 Slice the steaks into thin slices and put into a large
bowl. Add the prepared vegetables and lime rind. Mix
the lime juice with the rest of the dressing ingredients
(in a jam jar is easiest). Just before serving, pour the
dressing over the salad and toss well.

stilton burgers

1 lb (450g) best quality minced
beef

1 red onion

1 tsp dried mixed herbs

1 tsp Dijon mustard

3 oz (75g) Stilton cheese

Salt and pepper

4 burger buns

Oven:

Floor of roasting oven

Prepare in advance:

Make the burgers and keep them
in the fridge for 24 hours before
cooking

Prepare ahead:

Keep the cooked burgers warm in
the simmering oven or warming
oven for half an hour

Freeze:

*Yes, freeze the uncooked burgers
and cook when defrosted*

1 Put a griddle pan into the oven to heat up before you
start to make the burgers.

2 Peel and chop the onion – easiest in a processor!
Add the mince, herbs, mustard, cheese and
seasoning to the onion and process, to mix together.

3 Shape into burgers – four large ones or 8 smaller
ones.

4 Transfer the griddle pan to the boiling plate and add
the burgers. Cook for about 5 minutes on each side,
turning only once. Lift the cooked burgers from the
pan and allow to rest.

5 Split the buns. Heat the toaster under the boiling
plate lid for a minute, then toast the buns on the
simmering plate – toasting them more slowly makes
the toast crisper and less likely to get soggy from the
meat juices.

6 Serve the burgers in the buns, with salad and lots of
relishes!

hallowe'en mince

Serves 4 – 5

Base:

1¼ lbs (565g) best minced beef

1 clove garlic

1 tbsp smoked paprika

Salt

1 tin (400g) chopped tomatoes

1 tsp chopped lemon thyme

Topping:

1 oz (25g) butter

1 tbsp olive oil

2 onions

2 oz (55g) plain flour

¾ pint (425ml) milk

Salt and pepper

Few grates of nutmeg

3 oz (75g) grated cheddar cheese

2 oz (55g) fresh breadcrumbs

Oven:

Roasting oven, 200C, 400F, Gas 6 and simmering oven, 130C, 250F, Gas 1

Prepare in advance:

Keep the cooked, cooled mince in the fridge for up to 24 hours

Prepare ahead:

Keep warm in the simmering or warming oven for half an hour

Freeze:

Yes, defrost and reheat in the roasting oven for 25 minutes

1 Put the mince, garlic and seasonings into a large heavy based pan and heat on the boiling plate.

2 Stir about to break up the mince, then transfer to the floor of the roasting oven to fry for 5 minutes. Stir and fry for a further 3 minutes. Tip in the chopped tomatoes and thyme, stir well and return to the floor of the roasting oven to boil and reduce for 10 minutes.

3 Whilst the meat is in the oven, peel and slice the onions. Melt the butter with the oil in a pan on the simmering plate and add the onions, stirring to coat. Heat until sizzling, then cover and put into the simmering oven for 15 minutes to soften.

4 Remove the meat from the oven and tip into a wide, fairly shallow ovenproof dish.

5 Take the onions from the oven, stir in the flour then the milk. Return to the simmering plate and stir until boiling.

6 Season well and, off the heat, add half of the cheese. Pour over the meat in the dish, then sprinkle over the breadcrumbs and remaining cheese.

7 Hang the grid shelf on the third set of runners in the roasting oven and cook the pie for 25 minutes until bubbling and golden.

braised beef

Serves 4

2 lb joint silverside of beef

2 tbsp olive oil

1 medium onion

1 clove garlic

3 medium carrots

2 sticks celery

2 tbsp horseradish sauce

1 tbsp plain flour

½ pint (275ml) stock, or stock mixed with wine

Salt and pepper

Oven:

Simmering oven,

130C, 250F, Gas 1

Prepare in advance:

The cooked beef can be chilled

and kept in the fridge for 24 hours

Prepare ahead:

The beef will keep warm in the

simmering oven for a further hour

Freeze:

Yes, defrost and reheat in the

roasting oven for 25 minutes

1   Heat the oil in a heavy casserole on the simmering plate, transfer to the boiling plate and add the beef. Move the pan to the floor of the roasting oven for a couple of minutes, then shake it to turn the meat over and continue to brown the meat in the oven for another 2 minutes.

2   Peel and slice the onion, carrots and celery, crush the garlic and add to the pan. Stir around then return to the floor of the roasting oven for another couple of minutes to brown, then transfer to the boiling plate, stir in the flour and horseradish, then the stock and seasoning and bring to the boil. Cover and transfer to the simmering oven for 2–3 hours.

3   Serve with mashed potatoes and a green vegetable.

marmalade cake

Serves at least 8!

  3 oranges

  8 oz (225g) caster sugar

  8 oz (225g) ground almonds

  6 eggs

Oven:

  Baking oven, 160C, 350F, Gas 4

Prepare in advance:

  Cook the oranges up to 24 hours in advance and keep in the fridge until you are ready to make the pudding

Prepare ahead:

  Keep warm on the edge of the Aga for up to an hour

Freeze:

  Yes, either completely cooked or just freeze the cooked oranges ready to throw the pudding together at the last minute

1. Put the oranges into a pan and cover with water. Bring to the boil on the boiling plate, cover and put into the simmering oven for 2 hours.

2. When the oranges are cooked, remove from the water and allow to cool a little.

3. Cut one orange into slices and set aside.

4. Cut the other oranges in half and remove the pips. Put into a processor and whizz, then add the sugar, almonds and eggs. Whizz again.

5. Pour into a lined 9" (23cms) cake tin (or the small roasting tin, lined with Bake-O-Glide). Lay the slices of orange on top of the batter.

6. *3 and 4 oven Aga*: Put the tin onto the grid shelf on the floor of the baking oven and bake for 35–45 minutes until set.

7. *2 oven Aga*: put the cake tin into a roasting tin and set onto the grid shelf on the floor of the roasting oven with the cold shelf on the second set of runners for about 25 minutes, then transfer to the simmering oven for about half an hour until set.

8. Serve warm or cold, with crème fraîche.

chocolate risotto

Serves 4

1 oz (25g) butter
2 oz (55g) pudding rice
2 oz (55g) caster sugar
½ tsp ground cinnamon
1 pint (550ml) milk
4 oz (110g) plain chocolate

Oven:

Simmering oven,
130C, 250F, Gas 1

Prepare in advance:

Cook, cool and keep in the fridge
for up to 24 hours, reheat in
simmering oven for an hour

Prepare ahead:

Keep warm in the simmering or
warming oven for an extra hour or
so, it will continue to cook and
thicken

Freeze:

Not this one!

1 Put the butter into an ovenproof dish and set on the back of the Aga to melt. Put the grid shelf on the floor of the roasting oven.

2 Put the rice, sugar, cinnamon and milk into the buttery dish and set on the grid shelf in the roasting oven for 5 minutes, then stir in the chocolate until it has melted. Return to the roasting oven for 10 minutes until boiling, then transfer to the simmering oven for 2 hours, until all the milk has been absorbed.

(For a faster pudding, use flaked rice and cook for an hour)

barbados bananas

Serves 6

6 bananas
1 tin (300g) coconut milk
2 tbsp Barbados rum
2 tbsp soft brown sugar

Oven:

Roasting oven, 200C, 400F, Gas 6

Freeze:

No, something VERY strange happens to the bananas!

1 Peel the bananas and slice them into an ovenproof dish. Pour over the rum, then the coconut milk.

2 Sprinkle with the sugar and bake on the grid shelf on the floor of the roasting oven for 25 minutes.

3 Serve with more rum!

barbados bananas *continued*

Prepare in advance:

Chuck the dish together and keep
in the fridge for up to 24 hours
before cooking it

Prepare ahead:

Will keep warm in simmering or
warming oven for up to an hour

plum *and* apple crumble

Serves 4 – 6

2 medium cooking apples

1½ lbs (600g) ripe plums

2 oz (55g) caster sugar

1 tsp ground allspice

6 oz (175g) wholemeal plain flour

3 oz (75g) butter

1 oz (25g) porridge oats

1 oz (25g) Demerara sugar

Oven:

Roasting oven, 200C, 400F, Gas 6

Prepare in advance:

Cook, cool and keep in the fridge
for up to 24 hours

Prepare ahead:

Will keep warm in the simmering
or warming oven for up to an hour

Freeze:

*Yes, defrost and reheat in the
roasting oven for 10 minutes*

1 Peel, core and slice the apples. Quarter the plums
and remove the stones. Grease an ovenproof dish.

2 Mix together the sugar and allspice, then toss the fruit
in the mixture. Pile into the prepared dish.

3 Whizz together the flour, butter and oats in a
processor, then tip onto the fruit. Spread evenly and
smooth the top. Sprinkle with the demerara sugar.

4 *3 and 4 oven Aga*: bake on the grid shelf in the
centre of the baking oven for 25–30 minutes until
golden brown

5 *2 oven Aga*: bake on the grid shelf on the floor of the
roasting oven for 25–30 minutes – you may need the
cold plain shelf for the last 15 minutes to stop the top
from browning too fast.

easter
pudding

Serves 6

4 hot cross buns

2 oz (55g) butter

2 tbsp marmalade

3 eggs

3/4 pint (425ml) milk

1 oz (25g) vanilla sugar

Oven:

Baking oven, 180C, 375F, Gas 4

Prepare in advance:

Mix together the pudding, cover and keep in the fridge for up to 24 hours before cooking

Prepare ahead:

Keep warm in the simmering or warming oven for up to an hour

Freeze:

Yes, cooked. Reheat in the roasting oven for 15 minutes

This also works well with 4 croissants, out of the hot cross bun season!

1 Split the buns in half and spread with the butter and marmalade.

2 Grease a 9" (23cms) square baking dish and lay the halves of the buns in it, overlapping slightly.

3 Mix together the eggs, milk and sugar and pour over the buns. Leave to soak for at least an hour, or overnight.

4 *3 and 4 oven Aga*: Put the grid shelf on the 4th runners in the baking oven and set the dish on it.

5 *2 oven Aga*: Put the grid shelf on the floor of the roasting oven and set the dish on it. Slide the cold shelf onto the second set of runners.

6 Bake for about 30 minutes until golden and crisp on top. Serve with pouring cream.

Keep vanilla pods after you have used them to make custard etc. Wash them then leave on the back of the Aga to dry, then drop into a jar of caster sugar to flavour it.

cranberry and orange pudding

Serves 4 – 6

6 oz (175g) fresh cranberries

2 oranges

4 oz (110g) butter

4 oz (110g) caster sugar

6 oz (175g) self raising flour

1 tsp baking powder

2 eggs

Oven:

Simmering oven,

130C, 250F, Gas 2

Prepare in advance:

Cook the pudding, cool and keep in the fridge for up to 24 hours. Steam for 30 minutes to reheat

Prepare ahead:

Keep warm in the simmering or warming oven for an additional hour or so

Freeze:

Yes. Defrost and steam for 30 minutes to reheat

Steamed puddings are the nuclear weapons in the battle of the sexes; produce one of these and you will be flavour of the month, if not the year!

1 Set the butter beside the Aga to soften for half an hour or so.

2 Grate the rind of the oranges and squeeze the juice.

3 Line a 2 pint (1 litre) pudding basin with cling film. We do want this pudding to turn out perfectly, after all!

4 Put all the ingredients – except the cranberries – into a bowl and mix thoroughly. Stir in the cranberries. Pour the mixture into the prepared basin and make a lid from cling film or clip on the lid if plastic!

5 Fold a sheet of foil into a strip and put the basin onto it. Put about an inch (3cm) of water into the bottom of a pan, (with a slice of lemon if it is aluminium to prevent the water from discolouring the pan), lower in the basin, put in the lid and bring to the boil on the boiling plate. Boil for about 5 minutes then transfer to the simmering oven for 2 to 3 hours.

6 When ready to eat, lift the basin from the pan with the foil then turn out onto a warm plate. Peel off the cling film. Serve with cream or custard (or both).

Once the pudding is in the simmering oven, you can cheerfully leave it for up to 3½ hours before eating, so go out and enjoy yourself while the Aga does the hard part!

variations on steamed puddings

You can make a steamed pudding from any sponge recipe, just tip the cake mix into a pudding basin and steam in the oven for a couple of hours!

blackberry and apple pudding

Serves 4 – 6

4 oz (110g) butter

4 oz (110g) caster sugar

2 eggs

6 oz (175g) self raising flour

1/2 tsp baking powder

1 medium cooking apple

4 oz (110g) blackberries

1 tsp lemon juice

1. Stand the butter beside the Aga to soften for half an hour.

2. Peel, core and slice the apple. Mix with the blackberries and lemon juice. Mix together the butter, sugar, eggs, flour and baking powder. Add the blackberry and apple mixture and stir gently.

3. Pour into the prepared pudding basin, cover the bowl and put into the pan with the water. Put the lid on the pan and boil on the boiling plate for 5 minutes, then put into the simmering oven for 2–2 1/2 hours.

4. Turn out, and serve with a dollop of crème fraîche or calvados-flavoured custard.

lemon curd pudding

Serves 4 – 6

4 oz (110g) butter

4 oz (110g) caster sugar

2 eggs

6 oz (175g) self raising flour

1/2 tsp baking powder

4 tbsp best quality lemon curd

1. Stand the butter beside the Aga to soften.

2. Tip two tablespoons of lemon curd into the prepared pudding basin.

3. Mix together the butter, sugar, eggs, flour and baking powder. Add the remaining lemon curd and stir to mix in.

4. Pour into the pudding basin, put into the pan with the water, put on the lid and boil on the boiling plate for 5 minutes, then put into the simmering oven for 2–2 1/2 hours.

5. When the pudding is cooked, turn out, and serve with a dollop of crème fraîche.

cape
brandy tart

Serves 6

1 tsp (5g) bicarbonate of soda

8 oz (225g) dates, stoned and chopped

¼ pint (150ml) boiling water

4 oz (110g) butter

8 oz (225g) soft brown sugar

2 eggs

6 oz (175g) self raising flour

4 oz (110g) pecan nuts, chopped

4 oz (110g) glacé cherries, chopped

1 ball stem ginger, grated

Sauce:

6 oz (175g) soft brown sugar

¼ pint (150ml) water

3 fl oz (100ml) brandy or rum

1 oz (35g) butter

Oven:

Baking oven, 180C, 350F, Gas 4

Prepare in advance:

Mix together a couple of hours in advance and cook at the last minute, or cook completely, cool and keep in the fridge for up to 24 hours

Prepare ahead:

Keep warm beside the Aga for up to 2 hours

Freeze:

Yes, defrost and sit the dish on the closed simmering plate lid to warm through for half an hour before serving

1   Set the butter beside the Aga to soften.

2   Put the dates and bicarbonate of soda into a bowl and pour over the boiling water. Leave to cool a little.

3   Beat together the softened butter, sugar, eggs and flour, and add the date mixture, pecan nuts, chopped cherries and grated ginger. Mix well and pour into a prepared 9" (23cms) baking dish.

4   *3 and 4 oven Aga*: Set the grid shelf on the floor of the baking oven and put the dish onto it and bake for 35–40 minutes until browned and set.

5   *2 oven Aga*: Put the dish into the large roasting tin and hang from the lowest set of runners in the roasting oven. Slide the cold shelf onto the second set of runners and bake for 30–35 minutes until browned. If not set, move the roasting tin, with the dish in, to the simmering oven for 10–15 minutes until set.

6   While the pudding is in the oven, put the sauce ingredients into a pan and bring to the boil on the simmering plate.

7   When the pudding is cooked, remove from the oven, pour the sauce over and leave to cool.

8   Serve tepid, with crème fraîche.

american
apple pie

Serves 4 – 6

Pastry:

8 oz (225g) self raising flour

5 oz (150g) Cookeen or other white fat

2 tbsp cold water

A pinch of salt

Filling:

1½ lbs (650g) cooking apples

4 oz (110g) caster sugar

½ tsp ground cinnamon

1 tbsp marmalade

½ oz (15g) butter

1 tbsp cornflour

2 tbsp orange juice

Oven:

Roasting oven, 200C, 400F, Gas 6

Prepare in advance

Bake the pie, cool and keep in the fridge for up to 24 hours

Prepare ahead:

Keep warm in the simmering or warming oven for up to an hour

Freeze:

Yes, defrost and warm through in the simmering oven for half an hour before serving

1   To make the pastry: Put the Cookeen and water into a processor and whizz. Add the flour and salt and whizz until it comes together as a dough. Wrap and chill until needed.

2   Peel core and slice the apples. Pile into a pan with the sugar and cinnamon and cook on the simmering plate until the apple is soft – about 10 minutes. Mix the cornflour and orange juice together and stir in, then boil. Remove from the heat then beat in the butter and marmalade and allow to cool.

3   Divide the pastry in half. Roll out and lay one piece on a pie plate. Fill with the apple mixture then roll out the rest of the pastry. Brush the edges with water and then put the second piece of pastry on top of the filling. Trim the edges and crimp together.

4   Cut the trimmings into pretty shapes and stick on top of the pie.

5   Sprinkle with caster sugar and bake on the floor of the roasting oven for 30 minutes until brown and crisp.

6   Serve with custard or cream.

mango and
passion fruit jelly

Serves 6, or more with another pudding

- 1 litre bottle mango and passion fruit crush
- 5 tsp (2 sachets) powdered gelatine
- 2 passion fruit

Oven:

Simmering plate

Prepare in advance:

Keep in the fridge for up to 24 hours

Prepare ahead:

Make the jelly 24 hours in advance but do not turn out until about an hour before you eat it, in case it goes splat

Freeze:

No, it melts very dramatically as it thaws!

1   Pour a little of the juice into a jam jar and sprinkle on the gelatine. Leave to stand for 5 minutes. Set the jar into a pan of water and bring to the boil on the simmering plate. Swirl the mixture round the jar occasionally.

2   Once the gelatine has melted completely, pour it into the rest of the juice and mix well. Pour into a prepared mould or glass bowl and chill until set, about 2–3 hours.

3   Just before serving, halve the passion fruit and scoop out the pips, which you then scatter over the jelly.

rhubarb fool

Serves 4 – 6

- 1 lb (450g) rhubarb
- 3 tbsp orange juice
- 2 tbsp sugar
- 7 oz (200g) tub mascarpone
- 7 oz (200g) tub crème fraîche
- 2 tbsp maple syrup

1   Turn the mascarpone into a bowl and set on the back of the Aga to soften.

2   Line the small roasting tin with Bake-O-Glide.

3   Trim and slice the rhubarb, then put it into the roasting tin with the orange juice and sugar. Hang the tin from the second set of runners in the roasting oven for 10 minutes until the rhubarb is tender and most of the juice has evaporated.

4   Tip the rhubarb mixture into the bowl of mascarpone

rhubarb fool *continued*

Oven:

Roasting oven, 200C, 400F, Gas 6

Prepare in advance:

Fool will keep in the fridge for up to 24 hours

Freeze:

Yes

and add the crème fraîche and maple syrup. Mix together thoroughly and chill for a couple of hours until set.

This method also works well with gooseberries for gooseberry fool.

damson cobbler

Serves 4 – 6

12 oz (375g) ripe damsons or plums

2 oz (55g) butter

4 oz (110g) self raising flour

1 tsp baking powder

½ tsp salt

7 fl oz (200ml) milk

8 oz (225g) caster sugar

Oven:

Baking oven, 180C, 350F, Gas 4

Prepare in advance:

Not really, it is nicest eaten the day it is made

Prepare ahead:

Keep warm in simmering or warming oven for up to an hour

Freeze:

Not this one, the damsons become watery as they defrost

1 Halve the damsons and remove the stones.

2 Put the butter into an 8" (20cms) square dish and put on the back of the Aga to melt.

3 Mix together the flour, salt, baking powder, milk and 7 oz (200g) sugar.

4 Pour this mixture over the melted butter. Do not stir! Scatter over the damson halves, then the remaining 1 oz (25g) caster sugar.

5 *3 and 4 oven Aga*: Bake on the grid shelf in the centre of the baking oven for 30–40 minutes until golden.

6 *2 oven Aga*: Bake on the grid shelf on the floor of the roasting oven for 30 minutes until puffed up and golden. You may need to slide the cold shelf onto the second set of runners after about 20 minutes.

7 Serve dusted with icing sugar and some cream.

To ring the changes, substitute half a dozen peeled, sliced peaches or nectarines for the damsons.

upside down pear and pecan gingerbread

Serves 4 – 6

Topping:

2 oz (55g) butter

3 oz (75g) soft brown sugar

1 tin (340g) pear halves in natural juice

12 pecan nuts

Cake:

4 oz (110g) self raising wholemeal flour

1 tsp (5g) bicarbonate of soda

4 oz (110g) soft brown sugar

1 tsp ground allspice

1 tsp ground ginger

1 egg

3 oz black treacle

¼ pint (150ml) milk

2 oz (55g) butter

Oven:

Baking oven, 190C, 375F, Gas 5

Prepare in advance:

Bake the cake, cool and keep in the fridge for up to 24 hours

Prepare ahead:

Keep warm in the simmering or warming oven for up to an hour

Freeze:

Yes, defrost and warm through in the simmering oven for half an hour

1 Line an 8" (20cms) square tin with Bake-O-Glide.

2 For the topping, put the butter into the tin. Set on the back of the Aga to melt, then sprinkle over the sugar. Drain the pear halves, and arrange the pieces, cut side down, in the tin and scatter the pecans around them.

3 Put the treacle, butter and milk into a pan and heat on the simmering plate until melted. Stir the dry ingredients together and add the egg, then the warmed treacle mixture. Beat well and pour into the tin.

4 *3 and 4 oven Aga*: Put onto the grid shelf on the fourth set of runners in the baking oven and bake for 40 minutes until springy to the touch.

5 *2 oven Aga*: Put the tin into the large roasting tin and hang from the lowest set of runners in the roasting oven, with the cold plain shelf on the second set of runners, and bake for 30 minutes.

6 Turn out onto a serving plate, leave to cool for 10 minutes then serve with crème fraîche or custard, or both!

cranberry and nut bake

Serves 4 – 6

12 oz (340g) cranberries, fresh or frozen

4 oz (110g) pecan nuts

6 oz (175g) caster sugar

2 eggs

4 oz (110g) butter

6 oz (175g) self raising flour

1 tsp baking powder

2 tbsp cranberry juice

1 tsp almond extract

Oven:

Baking oven, 180C, 350F, Gas 4

Prepare ahead:

Will keep warm for up to 1 hour

Freeze:

Yes

1   Grease a large, shallow ovenproof dish.

2   Set the butter beside the Aga to soften.

3   Put the cranberries and pecans into the bottom of the dish. Scatter over 2oz (55g) of the sugar.

4   Mix together the remaining sugar, butter, eggs, flour, baking powder, cranberry juice and almond extract, then pour this over the fruit and nuts.

5   *3 and 4 oven Aga*: Put the dish onto the grid shelf in the centre of the baking oven for about 30 minutes.

6   *2 oven Aga*: Put the dish onto the grid shelf on the floor of the roasting oven for about 25 minutes. You will need to slide the cold plain shelf onto the second set of runners after about 15–20 minutes to prevent it from browning too eagerly!

7   Serve dusted with icing sugar and some vanilla ice cream.

apple charlotte

Serves 4 – 6

2 lb (900g) cooking apples

2 tbsp sugar

1/2 tsp ground mixed spice

1 tbsp marmalade (optional)

1/2 oz (10g) butter

4 oz (110g) butter

6 slices day-old bread

Oven:

Roasting oven, 200C, 400F, Gas 6

1   Set 4oz (110g) of butter in a bowl on the back of the Aga to melt.

2   Peel, core and slice the apples. Put into a pan with the sugar, 1/2 oz (10g) butter, spice and optional marmalade. Cook gently on the simmering plate until the apple is sizzling, then cover and transfer to the simmering oven for 15 minutes to soften.

3   Cut the crusts off the bread. Cut two slices into large circles and the rest in halves. Brush with the melted butter and use one of the discs to line the base of a charlotte tin (or a 6" (15cms) deep cake tin). Line the sides of the tin with the half-slices.

apple charlotte *continued*

Prepare ahead:

Assemble and keep in the fridge for up to 24 hours before final cooking

Freeze:

Yes, cooked

4   Pile the apple mixture into the prepared tin and use the second disc as a lid. Press down firmly.

5   Hang the grid shelf on the lowest set of runners and bake the pudding for about 20 minutes until golden.

6   If you are feeling really brave, turn it out, before serving with a dollop of vanilla ice cream.

salisbury pears

Serves 6

6 medium pears

1/2 pint (275ml) red wine

3 oz (75g) caster sugar

1/2 pint (275ml) double cream

Oven:

Simmering oven,
130C, 250F, Gas 1

Prepare in advance:

Keep the cooled pears and sauce in the fridge for up to 24 hours, the sauce will thicken as it sets

Prepare ahead:

Keep close to the Aga for an hour or two before serving tepid

Freeze:

No, the sauce will separate as it defrosts

1   Peel the pears, leaving the stalks on. Using a teaspoon, gouge out the cores (or cut in half and remove the cores).

2   Put the wine and sugar into a pan on the simmering plate and heat until the sugar has dissolved. Add the pears and bring to the boil. Cover and put into the simmering oven and cook until soft – 25 to 40 minutes depending upon ripeness.

3   When the pears are tender, lift them out of the pan and keep warm. Put the pan onto the floor of the roasting oven to reduce the wine and sugar to about 3 tbsp (45ml) of thick syrup – this will take about 25 minutes, but keep an eye on it as it reduces, in case it boils away to nothing!

4   When the sauce has reduced, beat in the cream and pour over the pears. Serve warm or cool.

summer pudding

Serves 6

8 oz (225g) redcurrants

4 oz (110g) blackcurrants

1 lb (450g) raspberries

4 oz (110g) caster sugar

8 slices day-old bread

Oven:

Simmering plate

Prepare in advance:

Keep in the fridge for up to 48 hours

Prepare ahead:

Do not turn the pudding out until the last minute, in case it collapses all over the plate!

Freeze:

Yes, but defrost very slowly in the fridge, where it will give off quite a lot of juice

1 Put the fruit and sugar into a pan and gently heat on the simmering plate until the juice is running.

2 Remove the crusts from the bread and cut into triangles. Line a 2lb (1 litre) pudding basin with cling film and then with the slices of bread, reserving a slice for the lid.

3 Pour the warmed fruit into the lined basin. Trim the final slice of bread to fit the top.

4 Put a small plate onto the pudding and use a weight or full can to push it down. Cool and chill for 24 hours to allow the juices to soak the bread completely.

5 To serve, turn out, cut into slices and pour over lots of cream!

I have included this because I couldn't find a good recipe anywhere for summer pudding! A classic, this is popular with all generations.

blackberry mousse

Serves 6

1 lb (450g) blackberries

¼ pint (150ml) double cream

1 lemon

4 oz (110g) caster sugar

3 tsp powdered gelatine

2 egg whites

To finish:

1 lemon

Handful of blackberries

1 Grate the zest of the lemon and stir into the cream. Chill until needed.

2 Squeeze the juice of the lemon into a pan, add the sugar and most of the blackberries (reserving a handful for decoration later) and cook on the simmering plate for about 5 minutes until the juices are running and the fruit is soft. Either whizz in a processor or push through a sieve, then tip into a bowl.

3 Put 3 tbsp (15ml) water into a jam jar and sprinkle in the gelatine. Leave to soak for a few minutes, then put into a pan of boiling water to melt. Pour into the

blackberry mousse *continued*

Oven:

Simmering plate

Prepare ahead:

Keeps in the fridge for up to 24 hours

Freeze:

Yes, defrost overnight in the fridge.

This works with any soft fruit, raspberries, gooseberries, etc.

blackberry mixture. Mix well and allow to cool completely.

4 Whip the cream and fold it into the cold blackberries. Whisk the egg whites and fold them in. Pour into a serving bowl – or individual glasses – and chill until set.

5 Decorate with slices of lemon and the reserved blackberries.

raspberry mousse
ice cream

Serves 8

1 lb (450g) raspberries

$^1/_2$ pint (230ml) cream

2 egg whites

6 oz (175g) caster sugar

3 fl oz (80ml) orange juice

Prepare ahead:

Keep in the freezer for up to 2 weeks

Freeze:

Yes!

1 Line a 2 lb / 1kg loaf tin with cling film.

2 Crush all but a handful of the raspberries. If you are feeling keen, sieve them – this takes about 15 minutes with a wooden spoon and sieve, but it is worth it not to have to pick raspberry pips out of your teeth! Alternatively, just crush the berries.

3 Put the sugar and orange juice into a pan on the simmering plate and bring to the boil, then boil continuously on the simmering plate for 3 minutes.

4 Whisk the egg whites and then pour on the very hot orange and sugar syrup, still whisking. Whisk again for another couple of minutes until the egg whites are light and fluffy. Whisk the cream.

5 Fold the cream and raspberries into the egg white mixture, then pour into the prepared tin and freeze for at least 4 hours.

6 To serve, turn out onto a plate and remove the cling film. Decorate with a few raspberries and serve.

chocolate and
cherry fudge pie

Serves 6

6 oz (175g) plain flour

1 oz (25g) caster sugar

3 oz (75g) butter

2 tbsp cold water

14 oz (400g) tin or jar of cherries, or 8 oz (225g) fresh, pitted cherries

4 oz (110g) plain chocolate

2 oz (50g) butter

3 oz (75g) light brown sugar

3 eggs

Oven:

Roasting oven, 200C, 400F, Gas 6

Prepare in advance:

Bake the pie, cool and keep in the fridge for up to 24 hours

Prepare ahead:

Keep warm in the simmering or warming oven for up to an hour

Freeze:

Yes, defrost and reheat in the

roasting oven for 5–8 minutes

1 Set the 2 oz (50g) butter, chocolate and brown sugar in a bowl on the back of the Aga to melt. Drain the cherries very thoroughly.

2 To make the pastry, whizz the flour, caster sugar and 3 oz (75g) butter in a processor. Add sufficient water to bind into dough. Roll out and line an 8" (20cms) flan dish. Chill for at least half an hour.

3 Tip the cherries into the pastry case. Take the bowl of melted butter, sugar and chocolate and stir in the eggs. Pour over the cherries.

4 Bake on the floor of the roasting oven for 25 minutes. Serve warm.

Variations on this pie:

1 Substitute cranberries in season for the cherries for *Cranberry and chocolate fudge pie*

2 Substitute stoned damsons in season for the cherries for *Damson and chocolate fudge pie*

3 Substitute poached or tinned pears for the cherries, add some cocoa to the pastry, add some cream cheese to the filling instead of the melted butter for *Chocolate and pear pie*

4 Substitute white chocolate for the plain chocolate for *White chocolate and cherry fudge pie*

Roll out some pastry (see page 96) and line a 9" (23cms) ceramic dish and fill with:

prune tart

Serves 4 – 6

9 oz (250g) ready to eat prunes

5 tbsp brandy or rum

1 tsp vanilla extract

½ pint (285ml pot) double cream

1 oz (25g) caster sugar

2 eggs

1 Put the prunes into a bowl and pour over the brandy or rum. Leave to soak for at least a couple of hours, or overnight if possible.

2 To assemble the tart, mix together the cream, eggs, vanilla and sugar. Tip the soaked prunes into the prepared pastry case, pour over the creamy custard and set the dish on the floor of the roasting oven.

3 Bake for about 25 minutes, until the pastry is brown and the top risen a little and golden.

4 Dust with icing sugar and serve tepid with crème fraîche.

creamy apple tart

Serves 4 – 6

7 oz (200g) pack cream cheese

2 oz caster sugar

1 egg

½ tsp vanilla extract

1 tsp cinnamon

6 Granny Smith apples

1 Set the cream cheese on the back of the Aga to soften. Quarter, core and slice the apples. Peel them if you like – I prefer to leave the green skins on!

2 Mix together the cream cheese, sugar, egg, vanilla and cinnamon, then pour into the pastry case.

3 Arrange the apple slices in pretty circles on the top, then bake on the floor of the roasting oven for 25 minutes. Serve warm.

pecan and maple pie

Serves 4 – 6

4 oz (110g) pecan nuts

6 tbsp maple syrup

2 oz (50g) butter

3 oz (75g) light brown sugar

3 eggs

1 Set the butter in a bowl on the back of the Aga to melt for a few minutes.

2 Scatter the pecan nuts over the pastry. Take the bowl of melted butter and stir in the maple syrup, brown sugar and eggs.

3 Pour into the pastry case and then bake on the floor of the roasting oven for 25 minutes. Serve warm.

cheesecake tart

Serves 4 – 6

7 oz (200g) cream cheese

2 oz (55g) butter

2 tbsp caster sugar

1/2 tsp vanilla extract

2 tbsp cream

2 oz (55g) mixed dried fruit

2 tbsp plain flour

3 eggs

You could add a layer of stewed fruit between the pastry and cheesecake filling, rather than serving fresh fruit with it.

1 Set the cream cheese and butter for the filling in a bowl on the back of the Aga to soften.

2 Separate the eggs then beat the yolks, vanilla, sugar and cream into the butter and cream cheese. Whisk the egg whites and fold into the mixture, then fold in the flour and fruit.

3 Pour the filling into the pastry case and put onto the floor of the roasting oven for 25–30 minutes until the pastry is browned and the filling puffed up.

4 Serve either warm or cold, with crème fraîche and some fresh fruit.

apricot tart

Serves 6

1 pack (375g) ready rolled puff
pastry

1 lb (450g) apricots

1 tub (400g) mascarpone

2 tbsp caster sugar

1 egg

½ tsp vanilla extract

Oven:

Roasting oven, 200C, 400F, Gas 6

Prepare in advance:

Not really, best eaten the day it is
made.

Prepare ahead:

The tart will cool slowly for a
couple of hours.

Freeze:

*No, beware of the pastry going a
bit fatty*

1 Unroll the pastry onto a piece of Bake-O-Glide laid
onto the cold pain shelf.

2 Beat the egg with a fork and brush the outer inch
(2cms) of the pastry with the egg, then tip the
contents of the tub of mascarpone into the egg bowl,
add the sugar and vanilla: mix together.

3 Spread the mascarpone mix over the pastry, leaving
the border free.

4 Halve the apricots and lay them onto the tart.
Sprinkle with caster sugar then hang the shelf from
the third set of runners in the roasting oven for about
20 minutes until the pastry is puffed and golden and
the apricots just beginning to caramelise. Serve
warm or cold, dusted with icing sugar.

instant fruit sorbet

Serves 4 – 6

1 bag (500g) frozen mixed summer fruits

3 tbsp crème de cassis or Ribena

Prepare ahead:

Keep in the freezer for 1 week

Freeze:

Yes!!

OK, I admit this is not a recipe that demands an Aga in any way, but it is incredibly simple and really delicious!

1 Keep the fruit frozen until you are ready to make the sorbet.

2 Tip the fruit into a food processor and add the liqueur. Whizz until pulped, then turn into a freezer-proof box or bag and freeze for at least half an hour.

3 Serve in scoops, maybe in meringue or brandy snap baskets.

meringue baskets

Serves 4 – 6

4 egg whites

8 oz (225g) caster sugar

Oven:

Simmering oven,
130C, 250F, Gas 1

Prepare in advance:

Meringues will keep for up to a week in an airtight tin

Freeze:

Yes

1 Whisk the egg whites until stiff. Still whisking, add the sugar a spoonful at a time, until the mixture is thick and glossy.

2 Line the cold shelf with Bake-O-Glide. Either pipe into basket shapes or spread dollops onto the shelf, leaving a hollow in the centre.

3 *4 oven Aga*: Set in the warming oven overnight.

4 *2 and 3 oven Aga*: Hang from the lowest set of runners in the simmering oven for up to 2 hours, then set on top of the closed top plate lids overnight, to dry out completely.

chocolate and more chocolate terrine

Serves 8 – 10

½ pint (275ml) double cream

4 eggs

2 oz (50g) caster sugar

4 oz (110g) white chocolate

4 oz (110g) plain chocolate

5 tsp powdered gelatine

2 tbsp strong black coffee

3 tbsp orange juice or
orange liqueur

Sauce:

8 oz (225g) raspberries

2 oz (55g) icing sugar

Prepare in advance:

Keep in the fridge for up to 24
hours

Prepare ahead:

Turn the terrine out of its tin onto
a plate and decorate, then return
to the fridge up to a couple of
hours before eating

Freeze:

Yes, defrost in the fridge overnight

1   Set the two types of chocolate in separate bowls on the back of the Aga to melt. Line a 2 lb (1kg) loaf tin with cling film.

2   Put the coffee into a jam jar and sprinkle over 2 tsp of gelatine. Put the orange juice or liqueur into another jar and sprinkle over the remaining 3 tsp of gelatine. Leave for a few minutes to soak, then stand the jars in a pan of simmering water on the simmering plate, to melt the gelatine.

3   Separate the eggs and whisk the whites until firm. Whisk the egg yolks with the sugar until thick and creamy. Whip the cream.

4   Pour half of the yolk mixture onto the melted white chocolate. Fold together, then fold in the coffee and gelatine mixture, half the egg whites and half of the cream. Repeat this with the plain chocolate and the rest of the ingredients.

5   Pour half of the plain chocolate mousse into the tin and put into the freezer for 10 minutes, or the fridge for 20 minutes, until set. Then pour on the white chocolate mixture and return to the fridge or freezer until set. Finally, pour over the remaining plain chocolate mixture, smooth the top and put into the fridge for at least an hour until firm.

6   For the sauce, sieve the raspberries and stir in the icing sugar (or open a jar of raspberry coulis . . .).

7   To serve, turn out the terrine, remove the cling film and dust with icing sugar. Serve in slices, with a puddle of sauce on each plate.

This appears more complicated than it actually is and it probably takes longer to describe than to make, although it does use almost every mixing bowl in the cupboard! It makes a dramatic striped pudding and you can cut thinner slices to serve more people.

scarab beetle pie
(hazelnut and chocolate torte)

Serves 8

  2 egg whites

  3 oz (75g) caster sugar

  4 oz (110g) roasted hazelnuts

  1 oz (25g) plain flour

Filling:

  2 egg yolks

  1 egg

  4 oz (110g) caster sugar

  2 tbsp cornflour

  ½ pint (275ml) milk

  4 oz (110g) plain chocolate

  1 tsp vanilla essence

Oven:

  Baking oven, 180C, 350F, Gas 4

Prepare in advance:

  Make the hazelnut meringues up to 48 hours in advance and store in an airtight tin

Prepare ahead:

  Keep the assembled pudding in the fridge for a couple of hours

Freeze:

  Yes, defrost slowly in the fridge overnight

1 Mix together the egg yolks, whole egg, sugar and cornflour in a pan. Pour on the milk, stirring all the time, and heat on the simmering plate, still stirring, until it just comes to the boil. Remove from the heat and stir in the chocolate and vanilla until melted into the custard. Cover with cling film (to prevent a skin from forming) and allow to cool.

2 Line two loose-based 8" (20cms) sandwich tins with Bake-O-Glide.

3 Grind the nuts and flour together in a processor. Whisk the egg whites until stiff, then whisk in the sugar. Fold in the flour and nut mixture and pour into the prepared tins.

4 Smooth the tops and bake for 20–25 minutes until puffed up and browned.

5 *3 and 4 oven Aga*: set the tins on the grid shelf on the lowest set of runners in the baking oven.

6 *2 oven Aga*: put the tins into the large roasting tin and hang from the lowest set of runners in the roasting oven, sliding the cold plain shelf onto the second set of runners

7 Take the cakes out of the oven and turn out. Leave to cool. Line one of the tins with cling film and put one of the cakes into it, 'top' side down. Spread with the chocolate custard and gently lay the other cake on top. Chill for at least an hour.

8 To serve, take from the fridge and invert onto a plate. Peel off the cling film and decorate with whipped cream and some soft fruit.

hazelnut pastry torte

Serves 6

5 oz (150g) plain flour

8 oz (225g) hazelnuts

4 oz (110g) caster sugar

4 oz (110g) butter

1 egg yolk

½ pint (275ml) cream

¼ pint (150ml) Greek yogurt

2 tbsp maple syrup

1 pineapple or 4 peaches

Oven:

Roasting oven, 200C, 400F, Gas 6

Prepare in advance:

Make and cook the pastry discs and keep in an airtight tin for up to 24 hours

Prepare ahead:

The completed torte will keep in the fridge for up to 2 hours

Freeze:

The pastry discs yes, complete pudding, no

It is quicker to put this pudding together than to describe how to do it – once the pastry is cooked, it takes less than 5 minutes to complete!

1 Line the cold shelf with Bake-O-Glide.

2 Put the hazelnuts into a processor and grind them to almost a powder. Add the flour, sugar, butter and egg yolk and whiz together. You might need a spoonful or two of water to bind the pastry together.

3 Divide the pastry into three and press or roll each lump into a circle on the Bake-O-Glide. Hang from the third set of runners in the roasting oven for about 10 minutes, until golden.

4 Remove the pastry from the oven and allow to cool. Cut one of the rounds into six pieces, like a cake.

5 Whip the cream until stiff, then fold the yogurt and maple syrup into it.

6 Peel and slice the pineapple or scald, peel and slice the peaches, whichever you are using.

7 Put one of the pastry discs onto a plate and spread over half of the cream mixture. Lay half of the fruit slices on top. Put the next disc of pastry on top, then spread with the remaining cream.

8 Arrange the remaining fruit and the six pieces of the final pastry disc to overlap each other on top of the cream.

9 Sprinkle with icing sugar and serve.

summer fruits cake

Serves 10

5 eggs

5 oz (150g) caster sugar

5 oz (150g) plain flour

3½ oz (100g) white chocolate

1 pint (550ml) cream

1lb (450g) strawberries

8 oz (225g) raspberries

Few blueberries

1 tbsp rose water

1 oz (25g) caster sugar

6 oz (175g) plain chocolate

Oven temp:

Baking oven, 180C, 350F, Gas 4

Prepare ahead:

The cake will keep in the fridge for up to 24 hours

Freeze:

Yes, cake only

This looks really spectacular but is very easy to make. You might need a second pair of hands to help wrap the plain chocolate around the cake – especially the first time you do it, but be brave!

If summer fruits are out of season, try using green grapes and kiwifruit instead, and wrap the cake in white chocolate.

1 Grease and line a 10" (28cms) round cake tin.

2 Set the plain and white chocolate in separate bowls onto the back of the Aga to melt.

3 Break the eggs into a large bowl with the sugar and whisk until pale and thick – this takes at least 10 minutes! If you have a Kenwood or Kitchen Aid mixer, put in the eggs and sugar, turn it on and make yourself a cup of coffee then go and do the crossword until the mixture is fluffy!

4 Sift the flour and fold into the egg mixture. Pour into the cake tin and bake.

5 *3 and 4 oven Aga:* Set the cake tin on the grid shelf on the fourth set of runners in the baking oven. Bake for 35 to 40 minutes, until risen and golden.

6 *2 oven Aga:* Set the cake tin into the large roasting tin and hang from the lowest set of runners in the roasting oven, with the plain shelf on the second set of runners. Bake for about 25 minutes, until risen and golden.

7 Turn out and leave to cool.

8 For the filling: Halve half of the strawberries and place in a bowl with half the raspberries. Sprinkle over the rosewater and sugar and allow to macerate.

9 Whip the cream and fold in the melted white chocolate.

10 Cut the cake into two layers. Put the bottom one onto a serving plate, pile on half of the chocolate cream and then the soaked fruit. Put on the top half of the cake, then spread with the remaining cream.

11 Cut a strip of silicone paper to fit around the cake tin. Spread the plain chocolate onto the paper. Leave for a couple of minutes to begin setting, then wrap around the cake.

12 Chill for an hour until completely set. Remove cake from fridge, peel away the paper, tip the rest of the fruit into the chocolate case, sprinkle with icing sugar and serve to huge applause.

lemon and poppy seed drizzle cake

2 lemons

3 eggs

6 oz (175g) caster sugar

6 oz (175g) butter

9 oz (250g) self raising flour

1/4 pint pot (142g) natural yogurt

2 oz (55g) poppy seeds

1 oz (25g) granulated sugar

Oven:

Baking oven, 180C, 350F, Gas 4

Prepare ahead:

Should keep for up to 2 days in an airtight tin

Freeze:

Yes

Variation:

This cake will also work as a steamed pudding!

1 Set the butter beside the Aga to soften for half an hour.

2 Line the small roasting tin with Bake-O-Glide.

3 Grate the rind from the lemons into a bowl, add the butter, caster sugar, flour, eggs, yogurt and poppy seeds. Beat well.

4 Tip the cake mixture into the prepared tin.

5 *3 and 4 oven Aga*: Hang the tin from the fourth set of runners in the baking oven for about 30 minutes.

6 *2 oven Aga*: Hang the tin from the fourth set of runners in the roasting oven and slide the cold shelf onto the second set of runners and bake for 25 minutes.

7 Bake until risen and golden. Remove from the oven and allow to cool.

8 While the cake is cooling, squeeze the juice from the lemons into a pan and add the granulated sugar. Bring to the boil on the simmering plate then pour over the warm cake.

9 Serve tepid as a pudding or cold for tea.

pineappple cake

Serves 4 – 6

4 oz (110g) butter

4 oz (110g) dark brown sugar

6 oz (175g) self raising flour

1/2 tsp baking powder

1/4 tsp ground allspice

2 eggs

Up to 3 tbsp milk

4 oz (110g) glacé pineapple, chopped

2 oz (55g) mixed peel

Pineapple rings from a small tin

Oven:

Baking oven, 180C, 350F, Gas 4

Prepare ahead:

Should keep for up to 2 days in an airtight tin

Freeze:

Yes

Variation:

This cake will also work as a steamed pudding!

1   Line a 7" (18cms) cake tin with Bake-O-Glide. Set the butter beside the Aga to soften.

2   Drain the tin of pineapple and arrange the rings in a pretty pattern on the base of the tin.

3   Beat together the butter, sugar, flour, baking powder and eggs. Stir in the glacé pineapple and mixed peel and pour the mixture into the tin onto the pineapple rings.

4   *3 and 4 oven Aga*: Set the cake tin on the grid shelf on the fourth set of runners in the baking oven. Bake for 40 minutes, until risen and golden but still soft in the centre.

5   *2 oven Aga*: Set the cake tin into the large roasting tin and hang from the lowest set of runners in the roasting oven, with the plain shelf on the second set of runners. Bake for 40 minutes, until risen and golden but still soft in the centre.

6   Turn out onto a plate, dust with icing sugar and serve with cream or yogurt.

chewy chocolate brownies

Makes at least 24

3 oz (75g) cocoa

4 oz (110g) wholemeal self raising flour

13 oz (365g) caster sugar

10 oz (275g) butter

4 eggs

4 oz (110g) white chocolate drops

Oven:

Baking oven, 180C, 350F, Gas 4

Prepare ahead:

These will improve on keeping in an airtight tin for up to 3 days – if you can resist!

Freeze:

Yes

Variation:

To serve as a warm, gooey pudding, bake for a total of only 30 minutes

1   Set the butter beside the Aga to soften for half an hour.

2   Line the small roasting tin with Bake-O-Glide.

3   Pile all the ingredients except the chocolate drops into a processor and whizz to a paste (or beat thoroughly with a wooden spoon!). Add the chocolate drops and pulse to blend in.

4   Pour into the prepared tin.

5   *3 and 4 oven Aga*: Hang the tin from the lowest set of runners in the baking oven for about 45 minutes until browned but still a bit soggy in the centre.

6   *2 oven Aga*: set the grid shelf on the floor of the oven and put the tin onto it. Slide the cold shelf onto the second set of runners and bake for about 25 minutes until browned, then transfer to the simmering oven for a further 20 minutes until browned but still a bit soggy in the centre.

7   Allow to cool in the tin before turning out and cutting into squares.

cheese and
apple loaf

Serves 6

4 oz (110g) grated cheese

2 crisp eating apples

1 oz (25g) butter

2 tsp baking powder

1 tsp mustard powder

8 oz (225g) self raising flour

1 egg

Oven:

Baking oven, 180C, 350F, Gas 4

Prepare ahead:

Eat on the day of baking, if possible

Freeze:

Yes

This is a slightly different loaf, eaten as a savoury, not sweet, cake

1 Core and quarter the apples. Grate them, this is easiest in a food processor. Then add the rest of the ingredients to the bowl, change from the grating blade to the chopping blade and whizz to a dough. Knead briefly.

2 Lay some Bake-O-Glide on the cold plain shelf, and put the lump of dough onto it. Slash the top with a knife to show 6 portions, brush with beaten egg and bake.

3 *3 and 4 oven Aga*: Slide the shelf onto the fourth set of runners in the baking oven.

4 *2 oven Aga*: Set the grid shelf on the floor of the oven and put the cold plain shelf onto it, and slide the large roasting tin onto the top set of runners, to act as an additional cold shelf.

5 Bake for 35 minutes until risen and golden. Serve with soup or a salad.

blonde fruit cake

12 oz (340g) caster sugar

12 oz (340g) butter

4 eggs

12 oz (340g) self raising flour

6 oz (175g) ground almonds

4 oz (110g) cut mixed peel

4 oz (110g) glacé pineapple

4 oz (110g) chopped mixed nuts

1 tbsp brandy

Oven:

Baking oven, 180C, 350F, Gas 4

Prepare ahead:

Improves on keeping in an airtight tin for up to 1 week

Freeze: *Yes*

A lighter alternative to a rich fruit cake for celebrations or Christmas – just ice it as usual – or not!

1 Place the butter beside the Aga to soften for half an hour.

2 Line a 9" (23cms) round or 8" (20cms) square deep cake tin with Bake-O-Glide.

3 Beat together the butter, sugar, flour, eggs and almonds. This will make quite a stiff cake mixture.

4 Fold in the mixed peel, pineapple and mixed nuts. Pile into the prepared tin and bake.

5 *3 and 4 oven Aga*: Bake on the grid shelf on the floor of the baking oven for an hour then transfer to the simmering oven for a further hour.

6 *2 oven Aga*: put the cake tin into the large roasting tin and hang from the lowest set of runners in the roasting oven, slide the cold plain shelf on the second set of runners and bake for 35 minutes, then transfer to the simmering oven for 2 hours until a skewer inserted into the centre comes out clean.

7 Remove from the oven and allow to cool completely, then pour over a tablespoon of brandy and store in an airtight tin for a week before eating.

mango and citrus cake

1 tin (300g) mango pieces

12 oz (325g) mixed peel

2 eggs

4 oz (110g) softened butter

4 oz (110g) light brown sugar

6 oz (175g) self raising flour

Oven:

Baking oven, 180C, 350F, Gas 4

Prepare ahead:

Will keep in an airtight tin for up to 48 hours

Freeze: *Yes*

1 Line a 7" (18cms) round deep cake tin with Bake-O-Glide.

2 Set the butter beside the Aga to soften.

3 Open the tin of mangoes and drain. Tip the contents into a processor, with the butter, sugar, flour and eggs and whizz until mixed. Add the peel and pulse briefly to incorporate.

4 Pile into the prepared tin.

5 *3 and 4 oven Aga*: Set the tin on the grid shelf on the lowest set of runners in the baking oven. Bake for about an hour, until golden.

6 *2 oven Aga*: Set the tin into the large roasting tin and hang it from the bottom set of runners in the roasting oven, with the cold shelf on the second set of runners. After 30 minutes, transfer the roasting tin

mango and citrus cake *continued*

Variation:

This cake will also work as a
steamed pudding!

and its contents to the simmering oven to continue
cooking for another 45 minutes.

7   Turn out of the tin, allow to cool, sprinkle with icing
sugar, then serve.

raspberry muffins

*American-style muffin recipes are hugely fashionable, infinitely variable
and I have experimented widely with flavours! Children adore muffins
and they are so much easier to make than iced cup cakes!*

Makes 12

8 oz (225g) wholemeal self raising
flour or half and half wholemeal
and ordinary self raising flour

4 oz (110g) caster sugar

1 tsp baking powder

1 egg

1/4 pint (150ml) milk

1/4 pint (150ml) sunflower oil

4 oz (110g) raspberries – either
fresh, frozen or tinned

Oven:

Roasting oven, 200C, 400F, Gas 6

Prepare ahead:

Best eaten within 1 hour of
baking, or at least the same day

Freeze:

Yes, if really necessary

1   Line a large muffin tray with paper cases.

2   Put the raspberries into a bowl and crush them with a
fork. (If using tinned, drain them).

3   Put the flour, sugar and baking powder into a bowl.
Add the oil, milk and egg then stir very briefly to mix.
Stir in the fruit, and pour into the muffin cases.

4   *3 and 4 oven Aga*: hang the grid shelf from the
second set of runners in the baking oven and put the
tin onto it.

5   *2 oven Aga*: Set the grid shelf on the floor of the
roasting oven and put the muffin tin onto it.

6   Bake for about 15 minutes, until risen and golden.
Dust with icing sugar and eat as soon as they are
cool enough to handle!

More muffin ideas:

Add 4 oz (110g) chopped pecan nuts and a packet of white chocolate drops to the
basic muffin mixture.

Add a couple of tablespoons of mincemeat to the basic muffin mixture – far less
effort than mince pies!

Add a mashed banana and a couple of generous spoons of toffee sauce to the
basic muffin mixture.

Add a tablespoon of cocoa powder and a packet of plain chocolate drops to the
basic muffin mixture.

hallowe'en brownies

Makes 24

3 oz (75g) butter

4 tbsp black treacle

6 oz (175g) self raising flour

1 tsp baking powder

3 eggs

3 oz (75g) chopped pecan nuts

4 oz (110g) plain chocolate chips

Icing:

3 oz (75g) butter

1 tbsp black treacle

8 oz (225g) icing sugar

Oven:

Baking oven, 180C, 350F, Gas 4

Prepare ahead:

Will keep in an airtight tin for up to 48 hours

Freeze:

Yes

These can be served still-warm as a pudding, with some thick yogurt spooned over.

1   Put the butter and treacle into a bowl and set on the back of the Aga to melt.

2   Line the small roasting tin or Swiss roll tin with Bake-O-Glide.

3   Put the flour, eggs, baking powder, nuts and chocolate into the treacle and butter bowl and mix thoroughly. Pour into the prepared tin.

4   *3 and 4 oven Aga*: Hang the tin from the third set of runners in the baking oven.

5   *2 oven Aga*: Put the grid shelf on the floor of the roasting oven, put the tin onto it and hang the plain shelf from the second set of runners.

6   Bake for 25 minutes, until risen and springy.

7   Remove from the oven and allow to cool.

8   For the icing: Melt the butter and treacle together in a bowl on the back of the Aga. Stir in the icing sugar and mix well. Spread over the cake.

9   Cut the cake into 24 squares and serve!

Wipe the spoon with a little oil or butter before measuring the treacle, it comes off the spoon very much more easily.

christmas shortbread

Makes 24 pieces

12 oz (325g) plain flour

8 oz (225g) butter

4 oz (110g) caster sugar

Pinch salt

1 jar (340g) mincemeat

Icing sugar to finish

Oven:

Baking oven, 180C, 350F, Gas 4

Prepare ahead:

Will keep in an airtight tin for up to 48 hours

Freeze:

Yes

1 Line the small roasting tin with Bake-O-Glide.

2 Put the flour, sugar, salt and butter into a processor and whiz until the consistency of sand. Tip 2/3 of this into the tin and press down firmly – use the bottom of a tumbler!

3 Spread the mincemeat over the tin, then tip in the rest of the shortbread mix. Spread over and press down.

4 *3 and 4 oven Aga*: Hang the tin from the second set of runners in the baking oven.

5 *2 oven Aga*: Hang the tin from the lowest runners in the roasting oven – and slide the cold plain shelf onto the second set of runners after about 10 minutes.

6 Cook for 25 to 30 minutes until pale golden. Allow to cool before turning out, cutting into squares and dusting with a little icing sugar.

Other flavoured shortbread ideas:
This works really well if you use half a jar of raspberry jam instead of the mincemeat.
Try using half a jar of marmalade or half a jar of lemon curd instead of the mincemeat.

bread

You can vary your bread endlessly – tip in half a jar of sun dried tomato purée or pesto, some olives or chopped herbs, sesame or poppy seeds, use wholemeal or granary flour (which needs a little more water), use milk in place of the water, enrich it with beaten egg or saffron and fruit: the possibilities are endless!

Makes two small (1 lb/450g) loaves, one large (2 lb/1kg) loaf, or a dozen rolls

1½ lbs (700g) strong plain flour

1 sachet (7g) fast action dried yeast

2 tsp salt

$2/3$ pint (450ml) warm (hand-hot) water

Melted butter or beaten egg to glaze (optional)

Poppy seeds or sesame seeds to scatter over (again, optional)

Oven:

Roasting oven, 200C, 400F, Gas 6

Prepare ahead:

The dough will rise in the fridge overnight

Freeze:

Yes, once the bread is cooked

1   Put the flour, salt and fast action yeast into a bowl. Stir with a palette knife and mix, then pour in the water, still mixing with the knife – it's less messy than doing it with your hands! You may not need all of the water, use just enough to bring the mixture to a crumbly dough which will absorb the rest of the crumbs as you knead.

2   Tip the dough onto a board or work surface and start to knead. Think of traffic wardens, bad drivers, double glazing cold-callers, then take out your aggression on the dough, kneading well for about 10 minutes until it is soft and pliable.

3   Put the dough into a clean, greased bowl and cover with greased cling film or a piece of Bake-O-Glide and set beside the Aga for an hour or so to rise.

4   When it has risen and doubled in size – I think it feels like a baby's bottom at this stage! – turn it out of the bowl and knead lightly for about a minute, then shape into a loaf, loaves or rolls, and put into greased tins or on a piece of Bake-O-Glide on the cold plain shelf.

5   Glaze with melted butter or beaten egg and scatter over poppy or sesame seeds if you like, or not! Set on the grid shelf over the gap between the closed lids and allow to rise until it has once more doubled in size.

6   Hang the plain shelf (or the grid shelf with the loaf tins on it) on the lowest set of runners and bake for about 30 minutes for loaves, about 15 minutes for rolls, until the bread sounds hollow when you tap its base and the top is browned.

7   Allow to cool (if you can wait that long) before slicing and eating!

poultry stock

Makes 4 pints (2 litres)

Turkey, chicken or duck carcass once the meat has all been removed

2 onions

2 carrots

2 sticks celery

Sprig parsley

2 bay leaves

4 pints (2 litres) water

Oven:

Simmering oven,

130C, 250F, Gas 1

Prepare ahead:

The cooled stock will keep in the fridge for up to 24 hours

Freeze:

Yes, freeze in half pint pots for use in stews and soups

1 Put the bones into a large pan with the water. Cut up the onions, carrots and celery – no need to peel them!

2 Bring to the boil on the boiling plate then transfer to the simmering oven and leave all day or overnight until you remember that it's there.

3 Remove from the oven, strain off the bones and vegetables and allow to cool, then refrigerate.

4 When chilled, skim off any fat on the top, and freeze in small batches if not using immediately.

tomato purée

Makes about a pint (550ml)

2 lb (900g) ripe tomatoes

Oven:

Roasting oven, 200C, 400F, Gas 6

Prepare ahead:

Keep the cooled purée in the fridge for up to 3 days

Freeze:

Yes

1 Cut the tomatoes into quarters and put into a heavy-based pan.

2 Put onto the simmering plate until the juices have started to run, then stir and put, uncovered, onto the floor of the roasting oven for 20–30 minutes to reduce; keep an eye on it to prevent it boiling away to nothing!

3 Remove from the oven, allow to cool, then strain or process. Store in the fridge for up to 3 days, or freeze.

half cooked tomatoes

1 lb ripe tomatoes

2 tbsp olive oil

1 tsp caster sugar

Salt and pepper

Mixed dried herbs

Oven:

Simmering oven,
130C, 250F, Gas 1

Prepare ahead:

Will keep in the fridge for a couple
of days

Freeze:

Yes

1   Line the small roasting tin with Bake-O-Glide.

2   Wash the tomatoes and cut into quarters.

3   Lay them into the tin, with the skin side downwards. Sprinkle with the oil, then scatter on the sugar, salt, pepper and herbs.

4   Cook in the simmering oven for 3 to 4 hours, until about halved in size.

5   Allow to cool before storing in a jar in the fridge or freezing.

tomato sauce

Serves 4 – 6

½ pint (275ml) tomato purée (see p 118)

5 tbsp crème fraîche

½ tsp caster sugar

½ tsp balsamic or sherry vinegar

Salt and pepper

Oven:

Simmering plate

Prepare ahead:

Cooled sauce will keep in the
fridge for up to 2 days

Freeze:

Yes

1   Put everything into a pan and bring to the boil on the simmering plate.

2   Serve.

aga yogurt

1 pint (568ml) milk

1 tbsp live natural yogurt

Oven:

Simmering plate

Prepare ahead:

Will keep in the fridge for up to 2 days

Freeze:

No

I have experimented with adding powdered milk to the yogurt and the feeling in this house is that we prefer it without, but do feel free to try adding some with the live yogurt if you like.

1 Put the milk into a pan and bring to the boil on the simmering plate. Transfer, uncovered, to the simmering oven for 5 minutes for thin yogurt, 25 minutes for thick (Greek-style) yogurt.

2 Remove from the oven and allow to cool to blood temperature – when you put a finger into the milk, it does not feel hot! Stir in the live natural yogurt and pour into a dish or jug.

3 Cover then stand on a folded tea towel on the back of the Aga. Cover with another folded tea towel and leave for 6 hours or overnight.

4 Once the yogurt has thickened and set, cool completely and refrigerate until required.

sticky toffee sauce

1 tin (340g) condensed milk

Oven:

Simmering oven, 130C, 250F, Gas 1

Prepare ahead:

The cooled, unopened tin will keep in the fridge for up to 4 days

Freeze:

No need!

1 Put the tin, unopened, into a pan and cover with water.

2 Bring to the boil, then cover and put into the simmering oven for 2 hours.

3 Remove from the pan and allow to cool.

index

Aga baked tomato tart 15
Aga rice 26
American apple pie 87
Apple charlotte 92
Apple pie, American 87
Apricot tart 100
Asparagus and pea soup 10
Aubergine and potato curry 34

Bacon kedgeree 70
Baked beans wth bacon 65
Baked pudding, cranberry and nut 92
Baked rice with salmon 42
Banana and toffee muffins 113
Bananas, baked 80
Barbados bananas 80
Bean and vegetable stew 20
Beans, baked 65
Beef with molasses 74
Beef, braised 77
Beef, Hallowe'en mince 76
Beef, roast 46
Blackberry and apple pudding 84
Blackberry mousse 94
Blonde fruit cake 112
Boston baked beans with bacon 65
Braised beef 77
Braised lamb Bretonne 50
Bread 117
Brownies, chocolate 110
Brownies, Hallowe'en 114
Burgers, stilton and beef 75

Cake, blonde fruit 112
Cake, lemon and poppyseed 108
Cake, mango and citrus 112
Cake, marmalade 78
Cake, pineapple 109
Cake, summer fruits 106
Cape brandy tart 86
Caramel pear salad 4
Casserole, turkey 60
Cheese and apple loaf 111
Cheese tart 18
Cheesecake tart 99
Chestnut, gorgonzola and sorrel tart 19
Chestnut, mushroom and sage pasta 24
Chewy chocolate brownies 110
Chicken roulade with tarragon cream 2
Chicken with lavender and honey 63
Chicken, roast 46

Chicken, spicy Moroccan lemon 62
Chicken, spiked 62
Chicken, stir fried satay 64
Chicken, Thai coconut 58
Chicken, with lapsang 61
Chocolate and cherry fudge pie 96
Chocolate chip muffins 113
Chocolate risotto 80
Chocolate terrine 103
Choux puffs 6
Christmas shortbread 116
Cobbler, damson 89
Cobbler, peach 89
Couscous and vegetable salad 16
Cranberry and chocolate fudge pie 96
Cranberry and nut bake 92
Cranberry and orange pudding 83
Creamy apple tart 98
Creamy fish pie 43
Creamy onion soup 11
Crumble, mushroom, leek and chickpea 21
Crumble, plum and apple 81
Crumble, ratatouille and lentil 28

Damson and chocolate fudge pie 96
Damson cobbler 89
Date, cherry and nut pudding 86
Duck with sour cherries 57

Easter pudding 82

Fish pie 43
Fool, rhubarb 88
Fruit sorbet 102

Gammon, baked 70
Garlic tuna steaks 38
Ginger pork mystery stir fry 66
Gingerbread, upside down pear and pecan 90
Gooseberry mousse 95
Gougère, leek and onion 22
Gravy 46
Guinea fowl and sloe stew 56

Half-cooked tomatoes 119
Hallowe'en brownies 114
Hallowe'en mince 76
Ham lasagne 72
Ham, baked 70
Hampshire sauce 71

Hazelnut and chocolate torte 104
Hazelnut pastry torte 105
Hollandaise sauce 39
Hot halloumi and grape salad 8
Hot prawn and mango stir fry 44

Ice cream, raspberry mousse 95
Instant fruit sorbet 102
Instant pasta 27

Jelly, mango and passionfruit 88

Kebabs, monkfish 38
Kedgeree, bacon 70

Lamb and walnut tagine 47
Lamb steaks with minty sauce 48
Lamb, braised Bretonne 50
Lamb, roast 46
Lamb, Turkish pilaf 52
Lamb, with lavender 51
Lapsang chicken 61
Lasagne, ham 72
Leek and onion gougère 22
Lemon and poppy seed drizzle cake 108
Lemon chicken 62
Lemon curd pudding 84
Lemon shortbread 116

Mango and citrus cake 112
Mango and passionfruit jelly 88
Marinated monkfish kebabs 38
Marmalade cake 78
Marmalade shortbread 116
Mash, stilton and potato 32
Meringue baskets 102
Mexican bean and vegetable stew 20
Mincemeat muffins 113
Monkfish and bacon roll 40
Monkfish kebabs 38
Mousse, blackberry 94
Mousse, gooseberry 95
Muffins, banana and toffee 113
Muffins, chocolate chip 113
Muffins, mincemeat 113
Muffins, pecan and white chocolate 113
Muffins, raspberry 113
Mushroom risotto 25
Mushroom soup 12
Mushroom stroganoff 29
Mushroom tart 19

Mushroom, leek and chickpea crumble 21
Mushrooms, soufflé 4
Mustard mashed potatoes 32

Nasturtium, rocket, strawberry and prawn salad 8

Orange sauce 68
Osso bucco 55

Parsnip and stilton soup 11
Pasta, chestnut, mushroom and sage 24
Pasta, instant 27
Peach cobbler 89
Pear and caramel salad 4
Pear and chocolate pie 96
Pear and leek tart 18
Pear, stilton and walnut tart 19
Pears in reduced red wine 93
Pecan and maple pie 99
Pecan and white chocolate muffins 113
Pesto mash 32
Pesto sauce 41
Pie, American apple 87
Pie, chocolate and cherry 96
Pie, chocolate and pear 96
Pie, cranberry and chocolate 96
Pie, damson and chocolate 96
Pie, fish 43
Pie, pecan and maple 99
Pineapple cake 109
Pink turkey casserole 60
Plaice fillets with lime sauce 36
Plum and apple crumble 81
Pork and ginger stir fry 66
Pork fillet with orange sauce 68
Pork with apricots and leeks 66
Pork with warm apples 67
Pork, roast 46
Potato and aubergine curry 34
Potato salad 31
Potato, celeriac and sweet potato mash 32
Potatoes, mashed 32
Potatoes, mustard mash 32
Potatoes, pesto mash 32
Potatoes, roasted 30
Potatoes, saute 33
Prawn and mango stir fry 44
Prune tart 98
Pudding, blackberry and apple 84
Pudding, cranberry and orange 83
Pudding, Easter 82
Pudding, lemon curd 84
Pudding, steak and kidney 73
Pudding, summer 94

Rack of lamb with lavender 51
Raspberry mousse ice cream 95
Raspberry shortbread 116
Raspery muffins 113
Ratatouille and lentil crumble 28
Rhubarb fool 88
Rice and tomato salad 26
Rice pudding, chocolate 80
Rich venison casserole 54
Risotto, mushroom 25
Roasted butternut squash soup 14
Roasted roots 30
Roasting meat 46
Rocket and tomato roulade 2
Root vegetables, roasted 30
Root vegetables, steamed 32
Roulade, chicken 2
Roulade, rocket and tomato 2
Roulade, salmon 2

Salad, couscous and vegetable 16
Salad, halloumi and grape 8
Salad, pear and caramel 4
Salad, potato 31
Salad, rice and tomato 26
Salad, strawberry and prawn 8
Salad, Thai beef 74
Salisbury pears 93
Salmon and asparagus with cheat's hollandaise 39
Salmon en croûte 35
Salmon, baked with rice 42
Satay chicken 64
Sauce, Hampshire 71
Sauce, hollandaise 39
Sauce, orange 68
Sauce, sticky toffee 120
Sauce, tomato 119
Saute potatoes 33
Scarab beetle pie 104
Shortbread, Christmas 116
Shortbread, lemon 116
Shortbread, marmalade 116
Shortbread, raspberry 116
Slow baked marmalade gammon 70
Smart mushroom soup 12
Sole with leeks and pesto 41
Sorbet, fruit 102
Soufflé mushrooms 4
Soufflé, stilton 7
Soup, asparagus and pea 10
Soup, mushroom 12
Soup, onion 11
Soup, parsnip and stilton 11
Soup, roasted butternut squash 14
Spicy Moroccan lemon chicken 62
Spiked chicken 62

Steak and kidney pudding 73
Steaks, lamb 48
Stew, beef 74
Stew, guinea fowl and sloe 56
Stew, Mexican bean and vegetable 20
Sticky toffee sauce 120
Stilton burgers 75
Stilton mash 32
Stilton soufflé 7
Stir fried chicken satay 64
Stir fry, ginger pork 66
Stir fry, prawn and mango 44
Stock 118
Stroganoff, mushroom 29
Stuffed peppers 5
Stuffed pork fillet with orange sauce 68
Summer fruits cake 106
Summer pudding 94
Swede, mashed with Boursin 40

Tagine, lamb and walnut 47
Tart, apricot 100
Tart, cape brandy 86
Tart, cheesecake 99
Tart, chestnut, sorrel and gorgonzola 19
Tart, creamy apple 98
Tart, mushroom 19
Tart, pear and leek 18
Tart, pear, stilton and walnut 19
Tart, prune 98
Tart, three cheese and poppy seed 18
Tart, tomato 15
Terrine, chocolate 103
Thai beef salad 74
Thai coconut chicken 58
Three cheese and poppy seed tart 18
Three vegetable mash 32
Tomato purée 118
Tomato sauce 119
Tomato stuffed peppers 5
Tomato tart 15
Tomatoes, half cooked 119
Torte, hazelnut and chocolate 104
Torte, hazelnut and fruit 105
Tuna steaks with garlic 38
Turkey, casserole 60
Turkish lamb pilaf 52

Upside down pear and pecan gingerbread 90

Veal, osso bucco 55
Venison casserole 54

Yogurt 120